TOUGH
CRIME STORIES

2

TOUGH

A journal of crime fiction and occasional reviews.
www.toughcrime.com

Publisher/Editor: Rusty Barnes
Contributing Editor: Tim Hennessy
Associate Editor: Rider Barnes
Design: Sue Miller

ISBN-978-0-578-48780-9

ADDRESS:
Tough c/o Rusty Barnes
119 Bradstreet Avenue
Revere MA 02151

Contents

⟡⟡⟡⟡⟡

Itsy Bitsy Spider
Michael Bracken... *1*

The Third Jump of Frankie Buffalo
Thomas Pluck.. *18*

Day Planner
Matt Mattilla.. *26*

Tally Ho
William R. Soldan...................................... *34*

Beach Body
C.A. Rowland *60*

Viking Funeral
Nick Kolakowski.. *72*

Long Drive Home
Andrew Welsh-Huggins *78*

Masonry
Rob McClure Smith *97*

Once Upon a Time in Chicago
Tia J'anae *111*

The Grass Beneath My Feet
S.A. Cosby *117*

No News is Good News
Evelyn DeShane....................................... *124*

The Bag Girl
Alec Cizak.. *141*

Sarah, Sweet and Stealthy
Preston Lang... *149*

With Hair Blacker Than Coal
Chris McGinley... *161*

She Goes First
Mary Thorson.. *179*

Itsy Bitsy Spider

Michael Bracken

◇◇◇◇◇◇

I recognized Millie's work when I saw the tattooed spider web that radiated out from Mona's quarter-sized areola and covered her entire left breast.

"Where's the spider?" I asked.

A coy smile tugged at the corners of Mona Peterson's lips.

I found the spider later, tattooed at the edge of her bikini line, its eight little legs caught in her curly black pubic hair. By then, I was trapped.

Before then, though, I could have walked away. I probably should have.

◇◇◇◇◇◇

She first came to my office on a wet Tuesday afternoon, her college T-shirt glued to her like a second skin, and it was obvious she was both cold and braless. I tried not to stare at the dimpling of her thin gold T-shirt as she stood on the other side of my desk and dripped on my carpet.

Her hair hung in a sodden black mop and she tucked it behind her ears before she looked around my office. When she spied a stack of business cards on the corner of my desk, she pried one off the top. Neatly thermographed on the front of the card were my name—Morris Ronald Boyette—and my contact information. She held the card close to her face while she read. When she looked up, she asked, "This you?"

I'd just deposited a few thousand in my bank account—the final payment from a philandering spouse case I'd wrapped up less than a week earlier when I'd caught the husband on video sticking it to my client's sister on top of a picnic table in Cameron Park—and I didn't feel charitable. I said, "Yeah, it's me."

She dug into the front pocket of her tight-fitting jeans and dropped a wad of green on my blotter. I carefully peeled the wad apart, discovering five waterlogged Benjamin Franklins.

"I want to hire you."

◇◇◇◇◇◇

Millard Wayne Trout—Millie of Millie's Tattoos and Piercings—listened to the story over tacos and beer after he closed his tattoo parlor that night.

"She walked all the way from the university in the rain?"

"That's what she said," I told him between bites.

"Did you carry her back?"

"I offered."

Millie wore a gray sweatshirt, leaving only the tattoos covering his hands, fingers, and shaved head visible until he pushed the sleeves up to his elbows and exposed his thick arms. "And?"

"She said no."

"You see where she went?"

I shook my head. My office is a single room in the back of the building, behind Millie's Tattoos and Piercings. The empty suite across the hall from my office had once been occupied by a finance company too legitimate for the neighborhood and, in front of it, facing the street, was Big Mac's Bail Bonds. Without leaving the building, I could only see the alley behind the building and the empty lot to the side.

Millie drained his beer and opened another.

Someone tapped on the window and we both turned. Standing on the sidewalk outside were two young women—blonde, bouncy, and probably wasted. Millie walked to the front, unlocked the door, and pulled it open. He stood in the open doorway to prevent the women from entering.

"We're closed."

"No, please. Open up for us," said the taller of the two. "My friend wants a tattoo."

The shorter one reached in her pocket and pulled out a wad of money. "We can pay cash."

"Come back when you're sober, ladies," Millie said.

"She won't do it when she's sober," protested the taller one. She looked at her friend. "Show him where you want it."

The shorter blonde pulled down her tube-top.

"She wants it to say 'Got Milk?'"

"When you're sober, ladies," Millie repeated.

"We'll just go somewhere else!"

Millie eased the door closed. The two young women looked at each other while the shorter one pulled up her top. They staggered away.

Millie returned to the counter where we'd been eating. "Sober clients don't have regrets," he said. He poked through the wrappers and found the last taco. "I hate it when they come back crying."

◇◇◇◇◇

The next morning, after a quick Internet search and a few phone calls, I drove to the university and parked in one of the visitor lots. I hadn't been on campus in months and it took a while to wend my way through all the new construction. I finally found Mona's English professor in his office, half-hidden behind a pile of books.

He looked up when I closed the door behind me. "May I help you?"

I settled into the only unoccupied seat, rested my elbows on the arms, and steepled my fingers in front of my chest. "That depends."

"On?"

"How well you know Mona Peterson."

Color slowly drained from his face. "You related?"

I nodded. "We can trace our relationship back to Benjamin Franklin." Quintuplet Benjamin Franklins.

His eyes narrowed. "What did she tell you?"

"What matters is what I tell you," I said. "You don't contact Mona again. She gets an A in your course. I hear different, I come back to visit you."

He sat up a little straighter. "You can't do anything to me," he said. "I have tenure."

"You might keep your tenure," I explained, "but you won't keep your balls."

I let myself out of his office and returned to my Chevy.

◇◇◇◇◇◇

Lester Beeson had taken over Big Mac's Bail Bonds twenty-seven years earlier when a disgruntled client emptied a shotgun in Macdonald Pearson's face. Lester was sitting behind his desk thumbing through a stack of file folders when I stepped into his office. He looked up, saw me, and pulled a folder from the middle of the stack. He tossed it across the desk.

"This guy's become a pain in my ass."

I flipped the folder open and looked at an average Joe, the kind of guy who worked every minute of overtime the company offered so he could pay for the bass boat he used as an excuse to get away from some shrew of a wife.

"His name's Carl Weaver. He lives with his wife in Hubbard." Lester gave me the address. "He don't answer when I call, and the employer I have listed in his file says he ain't shown up for work in a month."

"And?"

"I need to see him in my office. I want some reassurance that he hasn't skipped."

◇◇◇◇◇◇

Millie left his shop in the capable hands of Alice Frizell, a wisp of a tattoo artist he'd hired a year earlier, and he rode with me to Hubbard, a small town about thirty miles northeast of Waco.

Weaver lived in a one-bedroom frame house near the cemetery, and only one car occupied the driveway. I dropped Millie in the alley where he could watch the back of the house, and I found a convenient place to watch the front.

Weaver arrived home nearly an hour later, parked his pickup truck next to the car, and went inside. Thirty minutes later, his wife exited the house, climbed into her car, and drove away.

I called Millie's cellphone. When he answered, I said, "He's alone in there. Let's go get him."

"About time," Millie responded. "I'm freezing my ass off out here."

I went through the front door and Millie came in through the back. We met in the living room and quickly realized we were alone in the house. We discovered why when we found the clothes Weaver had been wearing strewn across the bed, three wig stands—only two of which held wigs—on the dresser, and a selection of women's clothes suitable for a large woman or a man of Weaver's size.

"Think he's really married?" Millie asked.

Although we found a lot of make-up, we found no feminine products. "If he ever was," I said, "he isn't now."

Millie and I left things pretty much as we found them and walked out to my Chevy. We drove to a small cafe, ordered cheeseburgers, fries, and coffee. While we ate, a young couple sat at a table near us. The woman wore low-slung jeans that exposed the T-bar of her thong and the tramp stamp above the crack of her ass.

Millie jerked his thumb at the woman's tattoo. "Whoever did that should break all his needles and quit the business. I do better work when I'm blind drunk."

"Why do they do it?"

"People get tattoos for all sorts of reasons," Millie said. "I do a lot of ugly people who would be better off spending the money on dental work and plastic surgery. And I do eighteen-year-olds rebelling against their parents who will probably regret it when they grow up to be soccer moms and Boy Scout dads."

I looked at Millie. Every part of his body that I had ever seen, except his face and his palms, was covered with tattoos. I wondered where he fit in.

After we finished dinner, Millie and I returned to Weaver's house. We waited in my Chevy until Weaver's return at half past midnight, and we were tired and not in the mood for subtlety.

For a second time, Millie went through the back door and I went through the front. We caught Weaver standing in his bedroom wearing only a bra and panties. He tried to resist until Millie planted a fist in his gut. We threw a blanket over him and grabbed some clothes. We walked him to my car, where he sat in back next to Millie and pulled on the clothes we'd grabbed for him.

On the return trip to Waco, I phoned Lester and told him we had Weaver. I said, "You could have told me he's a cross-dresser."

Lester laughed. "He must be one ugly woman."

"You don't know the half of it."

The bail bondsman met us at his office fifteen minutes later.

"How'm I going to get home?" Weaver asked.

"Not our problem," I told him as I left with Lester. I knew the guy probably wasn't going home, and where he was going his choice of underthings would not work in his favor.

After we left Lester's office, Millie slipped into his car—a 1965 Mustang he'd rescued from a junkyard—and I went home.

◇◇◇◇◇◇

Mona Peterson returned to my office at the beginning of the Christmas break. She carried a backpack and said she had no family with whom to spend the holidays. She said she wanted to thank me for taking care of her problem earlier in the semester.

I told her that the quintuplets had already shown their appreciation.

"The university won't let students stay in the dorms during Christmas break." I waited while Mona's gaze traveled around my office before settling on my face. "I can't go home and I can't afford a motel. I gave you all the money I had."

Clients always have sad stories or they wouldn't need to hire guys like me. "I don't give refunds."

"No," she said. "I suppose not. I wouldn't ask for one."

I waited.

"It's just that—" She sucked her lower lip between her teeth and chewed on it.

I knew where Mona was headed, and I let her lead me there.

"Do you know any place I might stay?"

I did. I had a two-bedroom brick ranch just off of New Road and I took her there. The second bedroom had become a large walk-in closet filled with storage boxes and dust bunnies, so I prepared a place for her on the couch while she showered. I used floral print sheets and a pink blanket I hadn't removed from the linen closet since my divorce.

After I finished preparing the couch, I retrieved a beer from the fridge, sat in my favorite chair in the living room, and nursed it.

When Mona stepped from the bathroom, she was wearing a white bath towel wrapped twice around her and was drying her hair with a second towel.

She looked at the makeshift bed and at me. "That's not what I had in mind."

Mona dropped one towel. Then she dropped the other. That's when I saw the spider-web tattoo that covered her entire left breast. I gagged on my beer. When I recovered, I asked, "Where's the spider?"

A coy smile tugged at the corners of my client's lips as she crossed the room.

I shifted position but couldn't hide my reaction to her nakedness. She straddled my lap and gyrated her hips ever so slowly.

One hand still held the beer. The other held tight to the arm of the chair. I said, "We shouldn't do this."

Mona continued gyrating her hips as she leaned forward and pressed her lips against mine. They were soft and parted easily to allow our tongues to meet.

I dropped my beer, wrapped my arms around her, and carried her into the bedroom.

When I buried my face between her thighs, I saw the spider, its eight little legs caught in her curly black pubic hair, so small I could only see it close up. Before I had a chance to react, Mona grabbed the back of my head and thrust her pubic bone against my nose.

I had not been with a woman her age since I had been a man her age. I had forgotten how energetic they could be, and we found several ways to pleasure one another. When we finished, Mona turned away, curled into a fetal ball, and fell asleep.

After I slid out of bed, I padded barefoot and naked into the living room, where I picked up the half-empty beer bottle I'd dropped before carrying Mona to bed. I used an old towel to soak up the spilled beer. Then I opened a fresh bottle and drank it while contemplating the meaning of Mona's tattoo and the web she had spun for her English professor.

◇◇◇◇◇◇

I returned to the office three days later, did nothing most of the morning, and accepted Millie's invitation to lunch at the wing place down the street.

Millie stared hard at the blonde seated two tables away. "That's the perfect canvas," he said. "Smooth alabaster skin, nearly hairless."

I told him about Mona's spider web and that it seemed like his work.

"The spider web?" Millie said. "I've only done one like it, must have been a year ago, maybe two. The girl looked so young I made her show I.D. She came alone, paid cash before I started, and never once complained about the process. Some of those college girls can be real whiners."

"Ever see her again?"

"She came back once, a few months after I did the work, said she needed a place to stay during spring break. I was shacked up with Bridget at the time or I might have offered her the couch at my place."

"She's not satisfied with the couch."

"I wouldn't think so, not a girl like her," Millie said with a smile. Then the smile faded. "You didn't—?"

I nodded. "I've seen the spider."

"Moe Ron, Moe Ron, Moe Ron." Only Millie called me that, and this time the nickname fit. "She's not much older than your son. You should know better."

"I should."

"Where is she now?"

"I left her at the mall," I said. "There's no way I'm leaving her alone in my house."

"At least you got that part right."

◇◇◇◇◇◇

I needn't have bothered. Mona was waiting for me when I returned home that evening, sitting in my favorite chair with an open beer in her hand, wearing one of my shirts and nothing else. Only a single button kept the shirt closed.

"How many people did you rough up today?" she asked.

"None," I said. I didn't bother asking how she'd gotten in because the back door key lay on the coffee table next to the day's mail, and I knew if I checked my key ring I would be short one key.

"Well, you did all right by me," she said. "I checked my grades this afternoon. Straight A's."

Mona's English professor had come through. How she'd earned her other high marks I hadn't a clue until she undid the button and let the shirt fall open.

"I think we should celebrate."

◇◇◇◇◇◇

Lester Beeson caught me on my way to my office the next morning. "Weaver skipped again," he said. "He's in the wind."

I walked up front to find Millie collecting payment from a biker with a face like a Shar-Pei and a fresh tattoo depicting a winged unicorn flying over a rainbow. After his customer walked out the door, Millie explained, "Said it was for his daughter."

"Can you get free? Weaver's on the loose again and Lester's not happy."

Millie called to Alice and told her to take care of things. We were walking around back of the building to our cars when Mona showed up. She said, "I'm lonely."

"I have to go," I told her. "We have a job."

"I don't like being left alone," Mona said. "Let me go with you."

"You'll get in the way."

As she sucked on her lower lip, I glanced at Millie. He shrugged.

I said, "Get in the back."

She did, and soon we were headed north out of Waco. As we passed through Bellmead, I glanced at Mona in the rearview mirror. "Millie says he did your ink."

"How do you think I found you?" Mona said. "I saw your sign that night."

◇◇◇◇◇◇

We followed Weaver's trail until we found him sitting in a well-lit diner in Corsicana, dressed as the ugly broad he'd been when we first encountered him. When he saw us push through the diner's front door, he dashed into the women's restroom, a place Millie and I dared not go with so many people watching us.

"I'll go out back," Millie said, "make sure he doesn't climb out a window."

Mona didn't say anything. She just pushed past us and marched directly into the women's restroom. We heard a rather guttural scream of pain, and she came out a moment later with Weaver's blond wig in one hand and his scrotum in the other. On his tiptoes, Weaver minced along behind her.

The other patrons of the diner stared at the four of us, but none of them interfered as Millie grabbed the back of Weaver's neck and marched him out to my car. Mona followed. I grabbed Weaver's purse from the booth where he'd been sitting, dug through it, and tossed some money on the table next to his half-eaten meal. Then I joined the other three outside.

Mona sat in the passenger seat and Millie sat in back with Weaver. After I slipped into the driver's seat, I turned and looked at our collar. "You're costing Lester a lot of money," I said. "I won't be surprised if he tries to revoke your bond this time."

"He can't do that."

Weaver didn't deserve a response, so I started the car and pulled out of the parking lot, headed home to Waco. None of us spoke until we handed Weaver off to Lester Beeson, and we walked out of Beeson's office as he began reading Weaver the riot act.

Millie returned to his tattoo parlor and Mona followed me into my office. As I settled behind my desk, she perched on the corner and did that thing with her bottom lip.

After a bit, she said, "Christmas is coming."

"And?"

"What are you getting me?"

"A place to stay isn't enough?"

"You haven't even put up a tree!"

"How about we pick one out tonight?"

She liked that idea. "Maybe I should go home and rearrange the living room so we have a place to put it," she said. "Call me a cab, Moe Ron."

⬦⬦⬦⬦⬦

Later, over beer, I told Millie I couldn't stay long because I was going Christmas tree shopping. Then we talked about what had happened that afternoon, about how Mona had walked Carl Weaver out of the women's restroom.

"She's got hold of yours, too," Millie said.

I had been about to take a drink, but I stopped. "How's that?"

"What do you know about Mona?"

"She hired me to—"

"To scare off the previous man in her life."

"You think I'm taking advantage of her?" I asked. "I'm not in any position of authority. I don't have any impact on her grades."

"You don't? How'd she ace the English class?"

I lowered my beer.

"Maybe you aren't taking advantage of her," Millie said, "but she's sure as hell taking advantage of you."

I stared at him.

"Christmas tree shopping? Really?"

I glared at him for a moment before I pushed my chair back and stood. "I have to go."

He waved me away. "Make like an angel and bend over," he said, "'cause you know you're going to take it up the ass when this is all over."

⬦⬦⬦⬦⬦

Mona had moved some of the living room furniture, opening up space by the front window. She said, "I think a tree will look nice right there."

She was right, it did. That evening, after I had the tree secure in the stand, I dug through the closet in the second bedroom for ornaments I hadn't used since my wife walked out. I hadn't realized it at the time, but my ex had taken all the good ones, and what remained was inadequate to the task of decoration. I said something to that effect.

"That's all right," Mona said. "I think the tree looks fine."

I strung the only two strands of twinkling lights that still functioned, and we sat on the couch staring at them.

As she snuggled into the crook of my arm, I asked, "Why are you here? Why couldn't you go home for the holidays?"

"My father doesn't want me around. He says I get in the way."

"What does your father do that you get in the way?"

Mona didn't answer my question, but asked one of her own, "What about your son? Why isn't he here for Christmas?"

I had told her about my divorce, but not about my son. His absence was not by my choice, and I had long since come to terms with our non-existent relationship. I didn't let her question distract me from my questions. "And why couldn't you afford to go somewhere else when the dorm closed for the holiday?"

"I don't get my allowance until the first of the month."

"Allowance?"

"I have a trust fund," she said. "My expenses are paid directly by the trust, and once a month I get some walking-around money. This month, all of it walked around without me."

"What about friends? Couldn't you have spent the time with friends?"

Her hand slid up my thigh. "I thought you were my friend."

◇◇◇◇◇◇

Lester Beeson caught my attention as I entered the building two days before Christmas.

"Weaver hung himself."

"I thought you had his bond revoked."

"I did," Beeson said. "Jailers found him in his cell this morning. He was scheduled for sentencing today. He was looking at three to five inside."

"A man like him wouldn't last long."

"He must have known it."

I had never bothered to ask what Weaver had done because I wasn't paid to care. Even so, hearing of his suicide put a damper on my day, and my trip to the jewelry store later that day wasn't as exciting as I had hoped.

◇◇◇◇◇◇

The next afternoon, as I prepared to head home to spend Christmas Eve with Mona, a man built like a defensive lineman pushed into my office, interrupting my examination of the Christmas gift I planned to give her. When I saw the butt of a semi-automatic hanging in a shoulder holster beneath his unbuttoned jacket, I shoved the gift in my desk drawer.

He asked, "Do you know Mona Peterson?"

"That depends."

"Humor me," he said. He closed the door behind him. "Let's say you do."

"Okay."

"So now you forget her."

"Why's that?"

"Her father insists."

"And who's her father?"

He rested his knuckles on my desk and leaned in close enough that I could smell the onions on his breath.

"Mona likes to toy with stupid fucks like you," he said. "You get a piece of that young stuff and you think you're in love. She'll chew you up, spit you out, and replace you with another stupid fuck. I'm saving you the grief by taking her off your hands now."

I didn't appreciate being told what to do, so I made a move. I thrust my hand under his jacket and grabbed the butt of his semi-automatic.

Before the pistol even cleared leather, my visitor drove a fist into the center of my face, smashing my nose and driving me backward. If my office hadn't been so small, I might have crashed to the floor. As it was, the chair tipped backward and caught between the wall and the desk, leaving me waving my arms and legs in the air like an upended spider.

"I guess it's already too late for you." He peeled five Benjamins from his wallet and tossed them on my desk. "This oughtta cover your pain and suffering."

He was gone before I could right myself, and by the time I reached the front of the building he was nowhere in sight.

Millie stepped out of his shop and joined me at the curb. He looked at the blood still streaming from my nose and put the pieces together. "Your visitor left in a stretch limo."

"You catch the plate number?"

He shook his head. "No, but when the door opened I saw Mona sitting inside."

"Anyone else?"

He named a state senator whose last name didn't match Mona's. Before I could grasp the implication, he added, "Come into the shop. I'll get a wet towel and we can clean you up."

When I returned home that afternoon, Mona's backpack was gone. So were half the Christmas tree ornaments. I hung her gift from the tree—a ruby-eyed gold spider on a chain—and stared at it as the twinkling Christmas lights reflected eerily from its eyes. Then I drank myself to sleep.

◇◇◇◇◇◇

The Friday after Christmas, Millie and I were discussing tattoos and sharing nachos at George's, half-empty Big O's in front of us, when Mona's English professor stopped at our table. I said, "Yeah?"

"Was she worth it?"

I couldn't answer his question, not then, so he turned and walked away. I watched him take the arm of a woman closer to his own age as they pushed through the door.

Millie and I resumed our conversation about tattoos, specifically about Mona's.

I said, "That spider was pretty small."

"I've done smaller."

"Yeah?"

"The smallest tattoo I ever did was for a writer," Millie said. "He had me tattoo a period on his ass."

I didn't want to know why.

◇◇◇◇◇◇

The Third Jump of Frankie Buffalo

Thomas Pluck

◇◇◇◇◇

Frank drove the half-ton as fast as he dared up the rutted, snowy road. His breath plumed like a big shot's cigar in the frozen air. So cold that they had shoved their booted feet into the campfires to keep their toes from freezing solid and snapping off. Only thing colder than winter in Chosin was the fear deep in his gut. The two supply trucks sent before him hadn't made it to the front. Artillery or ambush, no one knew. Frank held it in second gear and swerved around a bend. A moving target's a hard target. A hard turn came up quick, one foot on the brake and one on the gas...

A horn blast broke Frank out of the reverie.

This wasn't Korea. He was in a different truck, on a different run.

Nerves.

He didn't wake up shivering anymore, but in a truck job, Chosin always came back to him.

He was stuck behind a stubby oil truck and a black new BMW at a railroad crossing. The traffic for the car wash and the flashing light ahead always made this a bottleneck, but it was the best way to get where he had to be. The tanker had stopped at the tracks, and the morning commuters were getting antsy.

Frank checked his Timex. Fifteen minutes, plenty of time to get the Mack cement mixer to Rifle Camp Road and hit the power pole. More than enough time to cut the fuel line and spill some diesel, shut down the intersection and keep Paterson's finest occupied, waiting for the HazMat crew.

Honk.

It was the guy in the black BMW, one car ahead.

"He's gotta stop," Frank said to himself. "Law requires it."

It was his job to know. The CDL in his wallet wasn't in his name, and his no-work job at the port rarely got him behind the wheel anymore, but he knew all the rules and could drive anything over 10,000 GVW like nobody's business. It was a safe job. Just another driver heading to the quarry who made the turn too tight. If he got cited it wasn't even in his name, but the memories of the Frozen Chosin tickled in his gut.

Young Frank had never made it to the front. He could've made that turn, nothing for a fearless driver who'd cut his teeth bootlegging for Longy Zwillman, the Jewish giant who ran Newark. The cold inside moved his hands for him. The belly-cold had jerked the steering wheel, made him dive out the door with his rifle. All Frank could do was watch the half-ton spill its load of ammo and survival K-rations as it tumbled down the jagged stone cliffside. He connected with a new unit and told himself the two drivers before him had probably done the same thing.

Honk honk. This time it was the lady in the minivan behind him. Striped uniform, probably a waitress at some diner.

The tanker didn't need to wait this long. Just pause, really. The fading paint on the back of the stubby little tanker read Hansen Fuel Oil, the kind a small business uses to fill up home tanks. It rumbled forward, then stalled out. Right on the tracks.

Now Frank got antsy, too.

The boys would hit the Loomis armored car in twenty minutes. All pros, longshoremen in name only. They'd stolen the cement mixer off a job site that had lost funding and sat dormant for months. They laughed when he signed on for the job. Old Frankie Buffalo wants in? When he could be collecting his pension?

The pension wasn't enough. The job was barely enough. The medical plan's pure gold but Dottie's cancer cost platinum and diamonds, gutted his stake after putting their three kids through college. Now his grandchildren were near college age, and his kids had married for love, not money. For money there was always Poppy Frank.

To show the boys he could still motor, he got in a little yard hustler and spun it in donuts around their fancy German cars, parking it with a controlled skid. They kept their mouths shut after that.

Still plenty of time. All he had to do was get past the tanker. He checked the mirrors. The minivan was right on his ass. He cut the wheel hard left and eased forward. If the BMW gave him an inch he could squeeze by. He tapped the horn.

The BMW driver gave him the Jersey salute.

A decade ago he would have taken the breaker bar from under the seat and shattered this cafone's windshield. Maybe taken the little snubbie he used to keep under the dash and rapped the guy on the head.

But he wasn't what he once was.

The merciless Chosin winter had made his feet dead as bricks if the temperature dropped below fifty, like this morning. He could put on some speed when he wanted, but it looked funny.

Frankie's gonna shuffle off to Buffalo, the dock boss had said. And it stuck, like those names always do.

Two guys got out of the tanker. Olive skin, clean-shaven. First thing he thought was trouble, then chided himself, remembering his grandfather telling him how the country hated Italians before he was born, because some were anarchists. They even lynched eleven Italians in New Orleans, after a Black Hand hitter whacked the police chief. So he didn't like to judge. Even though he was Italian, and a crook.

Frank honked again.

The Beemer driver pointed at the tanker with his Starbucks cup. "Hello? I can't go anywhere."

Frank inched forward. The BMW disappeared under his hood, but he knew these Mack Granites like he'd known his wife Dottie's body.

"You scratch my paint, I'm gonna—"

The lights of the railroad crossing blinked red. Train coming.

The BMW driver swore, then the car jerked back and forth, making no headway. He had pulled too close to the tanker in front of him, and now he was paying for it. Other drivers piled out of their cars.

They were running.

The Frozen Chosin cold spread through Frank's belly. Run, it said. That thing's gonna go off like a five hundred pound bomb.

Across the tracks at the car wash, Latino women stopped drying cars and stared.

Frank set the air brakes and got ready to shuffle. He jerked the door handle. Sorry boys, you're on your own. They'd probably get cornered and mowed down before they made it five blocks with the money. There was no getting away from a betrayal like that. Frank would just wait for the hitter to come plug him in the head while he was home alone in the recliner, watching Wheeler Dealers.

The cold made a fist in his gut.

Then he saw the drivers, even the BMW jerk, shouldering the rear of the tanker. Like they could move it! If it's got a full tank, good luck with that.

Then the diner woman pitched in.

Frank jabbed the horn. "Lemme push him," he hollered. They used these trucks like tugboats in the yard all the time.

"You can't get around the cars," one shouted back.

Frank put the Mack in low gear. The cement mixer was spinning on an empty barrel, just for show. With no load, he could push the tanker and the car in front of him, no problem.

Frank the hero, not Frankie Buffalo. The woman in the diner uniform smiled and waved him on. She had a smile that took over her face, like Dottie had.

He eased the pedal down and they moved out of his way.

The BMW driver grimaced as Frank crunched his bumper and mashed the front end into the oil truck. For a second they all gasped, then the brake pins popped and the strange little train of tanker, crushed Beemer, and cement mixer began to inch forward.

The striped railroad gates slammed down on top of the tanker. Just a few more feet...

One of the oil men reached inside the cab and came out with something small and black, like the grease gun Frankie had at Chosin. It sounded the same, as a burst tore through the work shirts and the gal's diner uniform and the BMW guy's fancy suit.

The train horn drowned out their screams.

Frank ducked and the windshield blew out. Rounds peppered the cab and pocked the seat. What the hell were they doing? Nobody robs trains anymore. This was a commuter train, the double-decker diesel to Secaucus Junction. No freight worth a hijack.

They weren't stealing. They were killing. Like the anarchists that Frank's grandfather had told him about. Like the psychos who'd brought the Towers down.

Chosin ice gripped his bowels. Held off by the warmth that the diner girl's face put in his heart. He'd seen the Towers built floor by floor, and like everyone else at the port that day, had watched helplessly from across the water as they crumbled into cigarette ash.

Nowhere to run, Frankie. Gonna shuffle off to Buffalo?

His feet were numb, but he would die standing on them.

No grease gun. Not even the old snubbie. Just a breaker bar, two and a half feet of rusted iron. Blunt as a screwdriver, but sharp enough. He'd seen fights with them on the docks. Ugly ones.

He mashed the pedal to the floor with his elbow. The Mack ground its gears and shuddered. Two more bursts rattled through the engine compartment. Frank curled into himself, the cold moving his body for him again.

Steam hissed from a cut hose with the sweet stink of coolant, but the Mack kept nudging the tanker forward. The Mack's front end rocked as it rolled over the tracks. Halfway there.

Between the short, imperative blasts of the train horn came shouting, then the clank of a boot on the step by the driver side door. He gripped the breaker bar like a short spear, waiting for a head to pop up.

Four fingers gripped the door. Then the black barrel of the gun, wisping smoke.

Frank stabbed for the root of the middle finger and shouted words his nonno reserved for the anarchisti. Frank rose up for another thrust, but the gunner fell back onto the tracks, blood sprinkling from his hand like a pinhole leak in a garden hose. The train bore down on them skyscraper huge and swallowed the gunman, its brakes in full scream.

Frank jerked the door handle and tumbled out as the world spun and flickered like an old home movie.. The detached barrel of the cement mixer rolled toward the car wash. The rest of the Mack truck was dragged along by the train like a Tonka toy.

The brakes hissed as the train screeched to a crawl. Commuters gawped out the windows. The washers peeked from behind cars.

Frank curled up in the weeds clutching the breaker bar, like he had cradled his grease gun in the Korean winter.

The tanker had rolled ahead and butted into a wooden utility pole. Still close enough to the train to destroy it. The other oil man had the door open, bent over something.

Frank used the breaker bar as a cane and shoved himself to one knee. The killer swore to himself and jabbed at a little box behind the truck seat. Frank clubbed him in the knee, then brought the iron bar down until he lost his breath and the car washers covered their faces.

Frank saw what was behind the seat and dropped the bloody crowbar. Wires ran from a lockbox chained to the seat frame, out the door to the oil tank, which surely held something more volatile than heating oil.

Their backup plan.

Frank pulled himself into the cab and turned the ignition. Backed away from the pole and swerved, tires hopping, using the tank's heavy load as ballast for the turn. Like he was running with Longy Zwillman again.

He would make it to the quarry on Rifle Camp Road in time. He had to.

The boys hitting the Loomis truck would get more distraction than they would ever need.

And Frankie Buffalo would jump one last time.

◇◇◇◇◇◇

Day Planner

Matt Mattilla

◇◇◇◇◇◇

7:28 A.M.   The Chef shows up early again. The truck door slams shut heavy behind him. The Kid curled behind the outdoor heat grate might've been startled a long time ago but now he waits in patient silence for the footsteps to crack across the gravel and the kitchen door on the other side of the restaurant to close before he moves. Waits another minute as the Chef starts his prep. *Always wait for noises*, The Kid reminds himself. A minute of patience beats a whole day spent looking for a new spot. The Kid is careful when he creaks the grate open. Shoes are already on his feet when he steps on cold gravel. The cold air blasts him as he looks around the corner to make sure no one is coming and walks off to start yet another day on this Earth.

◇◇◇◇◇◇

7:32 A.M.   Jerry's a panhandler who does his thing on the highway off-ramp five minutes away. The Kid stands near him and helps make it look like they're a family or something. Sometimes drivers get all sympathetic and stop and fork a few bucks over. Jerry collects it in his old soda cup and splits the take with him but never shows him how much they both get which is bullshit. Three hours of this for five dollars. The Kid says thanks. They go their separate ways.

◇◇◇◇◇◇

10:37 A.M.   The coffee shop down the road is chill and doesn't ask any questions as long as he buys. The Kid waits in line with the other regulars. He avoids the looks. They don't mean anything to him anymore. They know what he is and he doesn't care. He is an outside animal trying to adapt to an inside world.

◇◇◇◇◇◇

10:39 A.M.   Line grows and lets him hide away in the middle of the herd. Let it grow. Let their faces melt into each other for the cameras and the workers behind the counter. Let him hide. The girl is on this morning, too. Her black hair tied back. Silver eyes darting across the coffee filters and cups and order sheets. *Don't look at her*, he begs himself. *Don't catch her eye. Of all people she'd be the first to say something. Give it a minute before you make a break.*

◇◇◇◇◇◇

10:42 A.M.   The bathroom door is locked behind him but The Kid is quick anyway with his cup-and-sink-water shower over the drain in the floor by the wall. Doesn't use too much soap. Keeps his ears open but a round of Q-Tips makes it hard. He brushes his teeth. Slicks his hair back and makes sure it stays under the winter hat. His clothes are from the donate box and don't smell that much after his last laundry session in a different sink last week. Jeans are black and don't stain. The layers he wears are interchangeable. It's cold out which means if anything gets dirty he can hide it till he has to wash it. He only carries what he'll need for the day in the bag and stashes the rest in a few trusted places hidden around the block. At first glance he is a college student without a car. Nothing else. Nothing is wrong. He is just in a place in between.

The Kid needs to stop staring in the mirror. Longer he looks the more he'll see wrong and the more paranoid he'll get.

Hurry up and get the fuck out.

◇◇◇◇◇◇

10:48 A.M.   Man in a suit waiting outside the bathroom door, face in phone.

It's good now, The Kid says to him, "Sorry I took a while."

Man looks up at him, grunts, looks back down at phone. Walks through the door. The Kid thinks the man knows what he was looking at or had already tried the door and he simply didn't hear it. The Kid tells himself to calm the fuck down. This is the worst time to get nervous. He moves around the tables in this back hallway where no one ever sits . In fact the only people sitting are up front with its big windows and neo-soul music echoing from the speakers behind the counter. The Kid thinks he knows this song. Might've liked it once. Three people in line get shuffled through easily. The Kid orders a large mocha latte, yes on the cream. She is the only one on duty. The Kid keeps his eyes on the back display and the menu and the counter and the stereo set on the nook in the wall.

Anything but her.

◇◇◇◇◇◇

10:50 A.M.   She stands at the other end with milk screaming in the steamer in front of her and his legs move closer to her while the rest of him follows along paralyzed. He stops himself at the counter, pulls his phone out, pretends to look at it. WiFi here means he can cruise through his social media and remember that there's a world outside of this fucking life. He doesn't have many friends, though, because he knows he could never bring himself to tell anybody. None of them would understand. They would fake their sympathy and look at him with pity for the rest of his life and when he'd man up and ask for help they would all say no. They always say no.

Phone's almost dead but the charger's plugged into the wall over there.

◇◇◇◇◇◇

10:52 A.M.   "Mocha large."

She sounds annoyed when she puts it down on the counter. Purple polish and chipped nails stay wrapped around it. He steps up. She hasn't let go. He doesn't go for it. Her other hand is hiding behind the machine. She's probably scared and doesn't want to show it. He's a monster from the forest who's come into town for a drink.

"Thanks," he says. Her head and the soft, bright face on it flashes from behind the corner. Her silver eyes are wide. She mumbles you're welcome and stares at him a second and then retreats behind the machine. She knows. Of all people for the love of God she knows. He says nothing else. He should be smart and get out but he grabs the cup and dashes over to the table. Safe. Around the corner. Hidden from prying eyes.

◇◇◇◇◇◇

10:54 A.M.   His coat still covers the bag and it is all undisturbed. He is alone in this section. He pulls old headphones he'd found on the ground a week ago out of his pocket. Finds the WiFi. Goes on YouTube hoping to find something good. *Just a few hours in this place*, he reminds himself, *and then move on*.

◇◇◇◇◇◇

11:34 A.M.   His legs are getting numb. The Kid needs to get up and stretch or they'll hurt like hell when he's outside again. The cup is half-empty. Luke-warm. He puts the phone back in his pocket and the coat over his bag and the charger under the table and trudges to the bathroom to pretend to piss. It's empty. He coughs again as the door slams shut behind him. His chest has been feeling heavy. His lungs vibrate like they're floating in water. He needs to get it checked out. He's smart enough to know a normal cough doesn't last for two weeks and clog his throat and take everything out of him. He needs to get it checked out. Jerry said it didn't sound good to him either. He needs to get it checked out. No insurance means no doctor but Jerry knows a guy at a shelter he stayed at once. He needs to get it checked out. He walks back to the table breathing in his nose and out his mouth like the medical website told him.

He sits down and takes a drink. It doesn't help.

◇◇◇◇◇◇

12:20 P.M.   The door chime is loud enough The Kid hears it from around the corner. There's heavy footsteps—boots—that go up to the counter. Kid cranes his neck up and looks through the window. No cop cars. Nothing in uniform waiting for him. He still has his headphones in but he hears the gasps and shushes clearly enough. He stays close to the wall and peeps around the corner. Boots is big. Boots has a mask on. Boots has a gun out on whoever's behind the counter. Another shriek. He retreats behind the wall and shoves his headphones in his pockets. Pulse thuds in his ears. No panicking. Boots is blocking the only way out. The shriek sounded female.

◇◇◇◇◇◇

12:22 P.M.   The thought clicks in place. *She's the only one here.* He is shook beyond all hell. If Boots shoots her she is close enough that she will die. Boots will come for him next. Boots shoots The Kid and he somehow fucking survives but has no insurance and he gets stitched up and sent back out on these streets with a bullet wound and a bill he will never be able to pay.

She's worth the risk. He has to do something. Boots hasn't seen him. His head's over the partition and The Kid is in his blind spot.

No point in not trying. He's overstayed his welcome here anyway.

◇◇◇◇◇◇

12:24 P.M.   The Kid steps towards him. His voice cracks but he hopes it sounds tough enough.

"There's nuh'ing in that drawer, man, says The Kid. Not past noon."

The Kid's voice quivers and time stops. The gun turns towards him—one swift, practiced motion.

"Shut the fuck up and get back."

The Kid stays put.

"Shooting won't help you none,"he finds the balls to say. His breath has stopped. His chest spasms and he thinks for a second that he'll never breathe again.

No time no time no time no time.

"The fuck you say to me?" Boots asks.

Boots charges forward, easy steps. Dark eyes all glossy. Dude's cracked. Desperate. Keeps asking the same question. The Kid throws his hands up and says nothing and never loses eye contact because some movie told him once that he shouldn't. No twitching. No coughing. Wait for him to get close and grab the thing.

Boots stops too far away.

◇◇◇◇◇◇

12:27 P.M.   Boots says the same line again. Behind him the girl is huddled on the counter holding a mop handle and giving The Kid a shhh. She's sly like a fox. Maybe she's seen the movies too. Maybe they could go see one together one of these days.

She moves with class, grace, bravery; all things The Kid knows he will never have. It's hard not to stare because the poor fuck knows he's in love but he also knows that'll tip the man with the gun off. Boots keeps chuckling under his breath, steps echoing on the linoleum. Kid still says nothing. Boots stops and keeps making tough talk.

Kid blinks and Boots takes a single hit to the base of the skull and his eyes roll back and he falls forward and lands with a thud that shakes the building. She puts her hands on her hips all triumphant and looks down at Boots then up at The Kid standing there in total awe.

"Thanks", she says, "for the help."

Kid shrugs. "Long as he didn't hurt you."

She smiles soft. Looks down at the body on her coffee shop floor. Stops smiling. Says: "Not the first not the last."

The Kid knows not to press it. He nods and looks down with her. Blue lights pull into the lot and The Kid tries not to panic.

"Finished with your coffee?" she asks, turning back.

"I'm just on my way out. I can take off now if you need me to."

She scoffs and laughs a little. "I'm asking if you want another one, dumbass. It's on the house."

Oh.

He shrugs. "Sure," he says, and she brings the mop to the door with her and lets the cop in.

"It'll just be a sec," she says to The Kid with a hint of white teeth. The cop stepping in behind her is all tall and big with a hard face and hands on his belt and The Kid nods at him. The cop nods back. Goes on his radio to call code numbers. Looks at Boots on the floor. The girl leaps over the counter and gets to making his mocha latte. Cop steps up and pulls a pad out and starts asking her questions. Boots stays on the ground with his gun far from his grip and a hand twitching.

The Kid walks back to the table wondering if his phone number still works.

◇◇◇◇◇◇

Tally Ho

William R. Soldan

◇◇◇◇◇

Gordon Jurewicz had just pulled into the parking lot of the Fortune Moon, as he did most nights after work, when the rear passenger door of his repurposed Crown Victoria was yanked open and a young woman scrambled in shouting, "Drive, drive!" A black, short cropped bob with platinum streaks framed her narrow features. Her face was battered, her voice frantic, and through the Valley Cab taxi's Plexiglas divider, she looked to Gordon no more than eighteen, maybe twenty. He was done for the night, wanted nothing more but to eat his Tuesday usual—a General Tso's combination plate with egg roll and soup—then go home to give his mother her medicine and retire to his basement room to watch a DVD. In fact, on some level, the present scene reminded him of one of his favorite films, but the thought was gone before it could settle into focus. He saw no one pursuing her, but the apprehension on her face made him tense, and he had no desire to find out what had her so scared.

So he drove, heading south toward downtown. "So where is it we're going?" he asked more than once, to which she always replied, "Just keep driving, okay?" He moved up and down the narrow one-ways off Federal and Commerce. Each time he looked back at her, she was checking her phone, texting, biting her nails. Though he knew she'd been beaten, he couldn't tell how bad the damage was; in the orange cast of the street lamps illuminating the backseat in swift intervals, it was hard distinguishing bruise from shadow.

"Who did that to you?"

She looked up for the first time to meet his eyes in the mirror, and that's when her expression of fear became one of indignation. At first he thought it was at the question itself, at the fact that he was prying, which is something he'd learned not to do with passengers. Part of a cabbie's livelihood in such a small city was dependent on his willingness to turn a blind eye and not ask questions. But she wasn't a usual fare, so he'd ventured out of character and meddled. Perhaps he'd live to regret it, he thought now.

But when she spoke, she did so openly enough. "I'll tell you who," she said, crying a little as she said it. "A nasty bastard who'd still be stripping copper out of houses and boosting car stereos if it wasn't for me, the limp-dick motherfucker."

Her phone buzzed and she read something on the screen, its cold, anemic light making her look like some lost spirit. And that was how he would go on to picture her after she jumped out of the cab at a red light and, without another word, vanished like a breath.

◇◇◇◇◇◇

The next morning, Gordon replaced the poison bait in the cage traps around the perimeter of the two-story farmhouse. Rodents had been getting in the garbage again. Coons, rats. He'd found several of each over the last few months, but they kept coming back. When he was finished, he went inside and gave his mother her insulin before driving to fetch her a half-dozen Boston Creams from the Plaza Donuts. Despite the diabetes and having already lost one foot due to an infected ulcer that had festered for too long, she refused to give up her sweets—the Ho-Ho's and Little Debbie's and two-liters of Pepsi. She weighed nearly four-hundred pounds and only got up from the king-sized bed upstairs to hobble with her walker to the bathroom.

◇◇◇◇◇◇

As she worked her way through the donuts, Gordon rubbed lotion on the foot that still remained, while the puckered stump of the one she'd lost pointed at him like a shiny, accusatory finger. She was by no means a loving woman, or even the least bit pleasant. There were days when he fantasized about leaving her there without her medicine, going about his day while her blood thickened and she slowly slipped into shock and then a coma, perhaps inject-ing her with a cocktail of some of his late father's leftover pain medication. There were Oxycontin and Percocet and Vicodin lining an entire cupboard shelf in the kitchen. But he could never go through with it. She was his own flesh and blood, after all. Besides, he figured she'd do herself in before long.

"Where's my damn cigarettes?" she barked, her voice like gravel in a tin can from decades of smoking two packs a day.

"I'll have to go back," he said. "I musta forgot."

"'I musta forgot,'" she mocked. "Christ, boy, you's about as useless as your father was. Least *he* had the sense to kill himself and put me out of my damn misery."

After the construction site accident, in which his father had shattered his pelvis and fractured several vertebrae, the man had slipped into a depressed state, eating his pills and retreating further and further inside himself until one day he took one too many, or perhaps the wrong combination of things, and never woke up. It was during times like this, though, that Gordon wanted to remind his mother that it was the settlement from his father's injury, and the life insurance policy he'd had the foresight to take out, that had paid off the mortgage and allowed her to sit around here getting fatter and meaner with nothing but her disability check coming in. Of course, most of the money from his father was long gone, and Gordon had to pick up the slack, but that was beside the point.

"Sorry, Ma," he said, slipping on her compression stockings before getting up. "I'll go now."

"Goddamn right you'll go now," she said. He was halfway down the stairs when she yelled after him: "And pick up some more damn Pepsi while you're at it!"

◇◇◇◇◇◇

The dining room of the Fortune Moon restaurant was deserted. This, along with the dim lighting, was one of the reasons Gordon came here. He felt much less self-conscious than he did under the fluorescents over at the Denny's on the other side of the highway. Tonight he sat in his usual booth in the back corner with a spread of egg rolls, fried wontons, sweet & sour pork, and chicken lo mein taking up most of the table in front of him. He knew he really shouldn't be eating so much of this stuff, at least not as often as he did. So far, he hadn't grown fat, not like his mother, but at thirty, his metabolism wasn't what it once was, and sitting behind the wheel of the cab all day didn't help. In the last few years, he'd gone from a fairly lean two-hundred pounds to a soft two-fifty, his once flat stomach hanging over his belt like a bloated udder. The grease was hell on his complexion, too, which was already pocked with acne scars from his unfortunate youth. Still, at least three nights a week, he found himself here, feasting alone in excess and telling himself this was probably as good as it was going to get.

◇◇◇◇◇◇

His shift was over for the night, though "shift" wasn't really the right word for it. He was an independent and worked as much or as little as he wanted, day or night. Each month he paid the Valley Cab dispatch service a fee to use their name and logo and provide him with customers. The car, a decommissioned police cruiser he'd picked up at a salvage yard was his; he owned and maintained it. Someday, he hoped to have enough socked away for a deposit on one of the vacant storefront properties down on Federal, maybe beside the pawn broker. He figured he'd be a one-man operation at first, but in time he'd get a few more cars and a few reliable employees to drive them. He'd only managed to save up about five grand since the idea first struck him, but within a couple years, he might just be able to pull it off. Until then, though, he had little control over the fares he was offered, only whether or not he took them when they came through on the radio, so he took what he could get, mostly drunks leaving bars or people traveling through on business, needing lifts to and from their hotels. But he got his share of crazies, too, people you'd never expect to have money, much less be willing to fork it over for cab fare—bums, crackheads. Now and then, everybody needed a ride, and in a forgotten town like this, the buses weren't always running.

He hadn't been fully aware that he'd been thinking about the young woman from two nights earlier until the bell over the restaurant's front door chimed and he looked up. She approached the cash register, and after exchanging a few words with the gray-haired Asian woman behind the counter, the woman disappeared into the kitchen through a swinging door. The young woman remained standing, and after a moment she sat on a bench between two potted bamboo trees and began playing with her phone.

Now that he saw her outside of the cab's backseat, Gordon realized just how thin she was. Sickly even, fragile enough to blow away in light wind. She'd been living rough, there was no doubt. Her bangs were pinned back, and even in the subdued light thrown by the gilded lanterns above the tables, he could see the discoloration around her eye and jaw.

She looked up and caught him staring. "Can I help you with something?" she asked, not unkindly. She had a slight drawl he hadn't noticed before. Kentucky maybe, or West Virginia.

He'd felt inconspicuous enough in the back corner, but now he felt exposed and awkward, which was more or less his usual state when in the presence of beautiful women, damaged or otherwise. "No, sorry," he said. "It's just, I wondered if everything was okay."

"Fine," she said. "Why wouldn't it be?"

"Well, you seemed more than a little freaked out the other night."

She seemed confused, but then there was recognition. "Oh, the cabbie, right? I didn't recognize you. Shit. Sorry about skipping out without paying, by the way. I was going through some things." She got up and joined him in the booth.

Finally he shrugged and said, "The meter wasn't running anyway. I was off duty."

She was amiable enough, but fidgety. The sleeves of her sweatshirt were pushed up, and he caught sight of several marks on her wrists and forearms, some of them scabbed over, some fresh and ringed with red.

"So anyway," she said, "thanks for the ride, I guess."

"Everything worked out then," he said. "You found somewhere to go?"

"I'm at the Tally Ho next door. Got a lift back after Damien cooled down. He was on the warpath again. Gets like that when he hasn't slept for a few days, but he tires himself out eventually."

"Damien," he echoed after a moment's hesitation. Here he was prying again. What had gotten into him? He'd never been one not to mind his own damn business. But something about her had him transfixed and wanting to know more. "Is he your pimp or something?"

She laughed so hard at this that it startled him, and he looked around, even though there was no one else in the place to hear her outburst. "Pimp? Jesus, man. Where the hell do you think we are? This is butt-fuck Ohio, not the Big Apple. Pimp. That's real cute."

His face grew hot. He'd made an assumption, based on the track marks and the fact that the Tally Ho Motel was a reputed nest of drug activity and prostitution—at least twice a year, he'd see on the news that the DEA or some other agency had done a sweep of the place—and he felt not only presumptuous now, but foolish.

"Sorry, wasn't my place to ask," he said.

"No harm, no foul," she said, and smiled at him. "He's just my boyfriend."

"He do that a lot?" Gordon asked, gesturing toward her face.

Her smile faltered, then she brushed it off like it was no big deal. "Just a misunderstanding," she said. "I shoulda known to let him alone when he was spun out like that."

He stopped himself before he could interrogate further, as much as he wanted to.

The old woman emerged from the kitchen carrying a takeout order with a receipt attached to it. She looked around when she saw the young woman was gone, and then she spotted her in the booth with Gordon. "Order ready," she announced.

The young woman got up. "I'm Haley," she said, but didn't offer her hand to shake.

"Gordon," he said, holding out his. She shook it. Her skin felt clammy but delicate in his palm.

"Nice talking with you, Gordon," she said, then started away, stopping after a few steps. She turned back. "Say, Gordy. You wouldn't have a few bucks you could spare, would ya?

◇◇◇◇◇◇

Haley. Ha-ley. The name made him think of comets tearing through space, burning bright and dying fast. He couldn't stop thinking about her. Another three days had gone by since he'd seen her at the restaurant, and he kept seeing her in his mind. The frail, abused figure. And that smile. He'd be driving a fare from the bus station to the Holiday Inn south of the city, or picking someone up from the sticks, and he'd remember that smile. It's not that women had never smiled at him, just that most of them had felt like pity smiles, those given by schoolteachers to children too dumb to learn. But Haley—there had been warmth in hers, something that expressed an unspoken connection between them.

◇◇◇◇◇◇

Finally he couldn't take it anymore. After picking up a twitchy couple, who'd crammed into the back-seat of his cab with a large flat-screen TV, and drop-ping them at the pawnshop downtown, he drove to the Fortune Moon. He parked and waited to catch a glimpse of her at the motel next door, passing up several calls from dispatch as he did so. After a few hours, however, he gave up, telling himself he was being ridiculous—she was just a junkie who'd needed a ride.

But the next day, he was sitting in his usual booth eating a Beef & Broccoli lunch special when he saw her crossing the parking lot with a plastic grocery bag. She returned to her room on the ground floor of the Tally Ho, and just the sight of her had made his stomach tighten, so he left his unfinished lunch on the table.

Outside, he watched from his cab as a man drove up about ten minutes later and knocked on the door. It opened and he entered, and after a minute had passed, a different man came out. Though he couldn't be sure, Gordon believed this to be Damien, a lanky guy swimming in an oversized T-shirt, with a shaved head and a scraggly red goatee. Gray tattoos, which from this short distance looked like some sort of contagious infection, patched his arms and neck. He stood with his knee bent, one foot against the brick wall of the building, smoking a cigarette. Then he walked to the edge of the parking lot, paced there for a while, came back. A half hour later, the door to the room opened and the man who'd gone in left. In the doorway, Haley handed something to Damien, after which he hurried up to a room on the second floor. When he returned a few minutes later, he went into the room with Haley. Gordon stayed parked there for some time, waiting, for what exactly he didn't know. They'd been in there for over an hour when Gordon finally started the cab and drove home to check on his mother.

Men came and went, and for days Gordon watched, feeling helpless, as she must have felt helpless, he told himself. It was the same routine, taking place every two or three hours: a man would come, enter the room. Damien would exit. He'd linger, smoking and talking on his phone, now and then crossing to the gas station and returning with a bottle in a paper sack. Thirty minutes would pass, sometimes more. He'd duck into another room after the man left, and he and Haley would remain holed up until the next round.

◇◇◇◇◇◇

Call him what she would, Damien was whoring her out. Gordon had no doubt. And despite how nonchalant she'd acted when he'd made the assumption, or when he'd asked her about the bruises on her face, he knew she must want help. Each time the door closed, he pictured her behind it, half naked on a seedy mattress, buried beneath the weight of some sleazy stranger, strung out and afraid. No one would submit to such a life willingly. The drugs, sure. He watched the news, understood that there was an epidemic, especially in the Midwest. He knew there was a lack of funding for treatment centers, certain politicians pushing for stricter laws, more prisons. He knew it wasn't as easy as just changing the course of your life. But if the right person . . .

The thought broke off. "And I suppose you're the right person." He scoffed at himself, a disgusted sound, much like the one his mother made when he forgot something at the store, or when he wasn't prompt enough with her foot lotion. "You can go just ahead and forget that nonsense," he said.

But he couldn't forget.

◇◇◇◇◇

Later that night, he parked at the Fortune Moon and walked over to the Tally Ho while Haley was inside with a large bearded man who'd driven up in a brand new Silverado.

Gordon was nervous, unaccustomed to such shady dealings, never more than a distant, passive observer. But all he had to do was think of her—*Haley*—and what she must be going through, and that steadied him enough to approach.

"You Damien?" he asked the guy outside.

Up close, he looked even rattier than he had from across the lot through the cab's windshield.

"Who the fuck's asking?" he said.

"Just heard you might have a girl. I've got cash."

His ears seemed to prick up at this. A flicker in his beady eyes.

"You sure as hell don't look like no cop, but who you been talking to?"

"Just a passenger. I drive a cab."

Damien looked at him skeptically, then said, "Fifty bucks for half an hour, hundred for a whole."

"That's fine," he said. "I guess I'll take an hour."

Damien checked his cell phone. "She's indisposed at the moment. Come back in fifteen."

Gordon nodded and returned to his cab. He listened to the static of dispatch on the CB and eventually shut it off. It was the longest fifteen minutes of his life. When the bearded man finally came out and left, Damien went inside and Gordon walked back over.

Haley opened the door. She looked exhausted but surprised. "Hey," she said. "What are you doing here?"

"Come in and shut the door," Damien said. Gordon did as he was told. Damien held out his hand, waved his fingers. "Money up front."

Gordon gave him a hundred dollars and Haley pulled Damien aside, whispering something to him. "It's cool," he told her. "Ain't gonna pass this up, are you?" She didn't reply, just looked down and shook her head. "Then I'll be upstairs. You can hold off a little longer, right?" She nodded, then he was gone, and Gordon was alone with her.

"So," she said, sitting on the edge of the bed. "What's it gonna be?"

At first, he didn't know what to say, though he'd rehearsed this moment all afternoon. He thought they'd just talk for a while, get to know each other a little, then he'd ease into it. But his nerves caused him to just blurt it out. "I want to take you some-where, away from here. Well, not take you away, just . . . I want to help you, I mean."

Her response was not one he would have predicted. "Man, you watch too many movies."

It was like a slap. "Huh?" he said.

"You want to help me, let's do this and get it over with, 'cause I'm not feeling too great right about now." She got up and crossed to the small table by the TV, started searching for something among a mess of wrinkled foil squares and empty cellophane wrappers.

"But, I don't understand," he said.

"That much is obvious," she said, and sighed. "Look, man—Gordon, right?—I bet you got some ideas about what life is like, driving around in that cab and all, but let me explain something to you. You probably think I run away from home 'cause Daddy touched me or something, and maybe Mama let him, right? Probably think that if I only had enough money to get to California or wherever that I could start over, finally go to college, get a nursing degree or some shit." She laughed. "Look, I'm sure you see yourself as a real noble guy. But this ain't prime time, Gordy. Get with the fucking program. There ain't no happy endings, only potentially less shitty ones. People do what people do, and I don't do shit I don't want to. Get it?"

"I didn't mean to . . . I didn't think that." Only he had. He'd fantasized about saving her, and she'd somehow reduced his entire sense of what things were like, of how they could be, into a plot summary, then pierced it with holes until it deflated.

"I shouldn't have come," he said.

"You paid for the hour," she said. "Take it or leave it. But we don't give refunds."

"I'm sorry," he said.

He got back to his cab feeling stupid and hollow. It was nearly 10 p.m. Again he wondered what the hell he'd been thinking. What had ever possessed him to believe he should play savior? Suddenly he pictured his mother at home, a shapeless mound in bed, chain smoking and gorging on cupcakes, her legs swollen, tight with fluid. He started the cab, turned on the CB, and listened to the calls coming through dispatch. He should really go on a few more runs, or just drive out of town and never come back. But she would need her medicine soon, and like always, he would be there.

◇◇◇◇◇◇

He'd just finished sponging the folds in his mother's back and was now massaging her shoulders while she shoveled fistfuls of chocolate-covered pretzels into her mouth and watched one of those competitive cooking shows. It was like kneading a slick lump of dough, and when his hands began to ache, he took to digging in with his elbows.

"Ouch!" she yelled. "Not so goddamn hard, you dipshit."

He'd been thinking about Haley and zoned out. "Sorry, Ma."

She grunted. "Ah, just get the hell off me if you can't do it right."

Normally, he'd apologize again and continue rubbing her down, but tonight he left her and went down to his room to pop in a DVD. He decided on *Taxi Driver*. He re-watched the film every couple months or so, never grew tired of it. And it seemed particularly appropriate tonight. When it got to the scene where a young Jodi Foster jumps into the cab because she's trying to flee her pimp, Gordon recalled the night a week previous, when Haley had jumped into his backseat, that sense of familiarity that had come and gone, and he found himself wondering: *What would Travis Bickle do?* It was laughable, but it seemed to cheer him up a little. *What indeed.* And the more he thought about it, the more absurd it was. First off, he would arm himself to the teeth. Gordon had owned a gun briefly, a .38 revolver, kept it in the cab for protection. But one night, he was held up at knifepoint while he was parked on a side street waiting on a fare. He'd pissed his pants and never even reached for the piece. The next day he went to firing range, hoping to get a little more comfortable with it. The booming sound of rounds exploding on either side of him made him panicky, though, and his hands wouldn't stop shaking, so he sold the .38 and got a stun-gun instead. Fortunately, he'd never had cause to use it.

Besides, he thought, Bickle was unhinged, psychotic. He plans to assassinate a presidential candidate because Betsy won't return his fucking phone calls, for Christ's sake. "Travis, Travis, what a kook," Gordon said to the screen. "But in the end? Nah, still a kook."

By the time the movie was over, he had a new perspective on his own audacity, how utterly dumb he had been. Whatever had driven him to try and interfere in the first place seemed vague and insignificant. She'd been right: this wasn't some drama in three acts, at the end of which the innocent are vindicated and all the villains slain.

This was the real world. And there were no happy endings.

He'd repeated this to himself, and had come to almost fully accept it as the hard truth when he came out of the Fortune Moon three nights later and found her sitting on the curb by his car, sobbing.

◇◇◇◇◇

"Haley," he said. "What's wrong?"

She looked up at him through bloodshot eyes, mascara running down her cheeks. Her lip had been split. A fresh mark had purpled her jaw. At first she didn't speak, just continued crying. Then she gained some composure and said in a phlegm-thick voice, "Hi Gordy, you got a minute?"

A light rain had begun to fall, so they got into the cab. She sat in the passenger seat, and in the close confines, the scent of her perfume or shampoo—something crisp with a name like Tropical Mist or Ocean Breeze, he thought—made his heart rate rise.

He let her be the first to speak. "I was thinking about before," she said. "About your offer."

A sudden rush spread through him, and he had a renewed sense that it had all been for a reason—her jumping in his cab that first night, his inexplicable meddling in things that shouldn't have concerned him. "I guess you had another misunderstanding?" he said, looking at the gash on her lower lip. She didn't appear to get his meaning at first, then understood and looked down, as if embarrassed. He said, "How can I help?"

"There's this place," she said. "Down by my folks, outside Lexington. A treatment center. There's a bed available, and . . .well, I just need a little cash for the bus ticket and to pay some up front deposit or something—you know, because I don't got no insurance?—and I'd ask Mom and Dad, but it's just Daddy's been out of work and . . ."

Her ramble trailed off and she looked out the window. The rain had picked up. It drummed on the roof. Fat drops swelled on the glass, broke, and ran down in jagged trails. She hadn't looked him in the eye the entire time. Of course not, he thought. She was desperate and ashamed. It made more sense to him now, why she'd been so frustrated and quick to refuse his help the first time—she hadn't been in her right mind. But she'd had a moment of clarity, however brief, and now she was here with him, asking for his help. Finally, her voice almost a whisper, she said, "I'm sorry, I shouldn't expect you to . . . you hardly know me, and I was such a bitch."

"Don't apologize," he said. "I want to help you. Just tell me how much you need."

Now she looked at him, eyes wide, so sad and sincere it made his heart hurt. "I don't really know," she said. "The bus ticket might not be that much, but the rest—maybe a few thousand? God, I know it's a lot. I understand if you can't."

He thought again of leaving and never coming back, and he wished he could just take her himself, but he couldn't leave his mother. This time, the realization filled him with a flood of resentment. He thought about how trapped he was, about the money he'd saved and how he really felt no closer to starting his own company. Five grand was nothing. It would help her a lot more than it would help him. Still, he needed to be reasonable. "I can pull together a couple thousand," he said. "Will that be enough?"

She straightened up in her seat. "Yeah, yeah that would be great," she said. "That would be fantastic, really." She began to ramble on some more about how she'd been wrong to snap at him and how the dope had her so mixed up, something about fate and how he must be some kind of angel. And he, too, had felt something had brought them together, felt it now more than ever.

"How soon can you get in?" he asked.

"Right away," she said. "I could go tonight."

He couldn't get the money until the bank opened in the morning, but he handed her what he had in his wallet to get some food. She looked unwell. It was only forty dollars, and part of him knew she'd buy drugs with it. But maybe she'd at least eat a little. If anything, he hoped it would keep her from having to turn tricks until he could come back for her.

"I'll be here by nine-thirty tomorrow morning to take you to the bus station," he told her. "You're making the right choice. Everything's going to be okay."

◇◇◇◇◇◇

The morning was overcast, but there was a brightness to it, the sky like a blank white slate that seemed to signal to him a new beginning for her, one he'd be a part of in his own small way. When she met him outside the motel, she had only a backpack and a purse, but didn't seem to be nervous. She said Damien was passed out, so there was nothing to worry about. "He's been speed-balling for a few days," she said, "but he finally ran out of steam. He'll be crashed out for a while."

"I really wish I could drive you there myself," he said as he pulled into the station and handed her the envelope containing two grand in twenty-dollar bills. There were people milling about outside the terminal doors, smoking and drinking coffee. A wino in camo pants and a trash bag poncho was yelling at a wall while a security guard chatted up a pair of young women waiting for one of the local buses. "Can I at least come in and wait with you?"

"That's really not necessary," she said. "You've done so much already."

He was about to insist that it was no problem when a call came in on the CB. A fare from the Marriott clear out to the Youngstown-Warren regional airport. Being two thousand bucks lighter, he told himself he couldn't afford to pass up the work. He hesitated for a minute, then answered the call.

"I don't know how I'll ever repay you," Haley said. "But I will someday, Gordy. I promise you I will."

"You just take care of yourself," he said. "That's payback enough."

She smiled at him, and he drove off, watching as she entered the building. He held onto that image of her leaving for the rest of the morning.

Once the ball had begun rolling, it all happened so quickly. Almost too quickly. She was gone, and he'd probably never see her again. But he was in high spirits, just the same. His fare to the airport, a distinguished, WASPy looking man in a suit that probably cost more than Gordon's cab, gave him a fat tip, and when he stopped back at the house to check on his mother, even her berating commentary couldn't bring him down. He was Travis Bickle without the bloodshed. This made Gordon laugh out loud. Sure, Haley had been only one young woman among many pulled into a world of degradation, but they'd found each other, and now she was free. He rolled down his window and whooped at a field of lowing cows on his way back toward civilization. "He was a kook, but they made him a hero!" he shouted, and a solitary bull looked up from munching grass to grace him with a disinterested stare as he passed.

He replayed it all from the beginning and was lost in a sense of redemption, not for her but for himself, of having made up for, in that one act, an unremarkable lifetime of disappointment and regret, of never being or doing enough. Even if no one ever knew what he had done, he would know, and *that* would be enough. Yes, it would be enough. He floated through this unwavering reverie all afternoon.

But there appeared a schism, like a stress fracture in the surface of his elation, when he was driving home.

"What the?" he muttered, and cut the wheel into the parking lot between the restaurant and the motel, pulling in front of her.

She jumped back, then turned, as if to run, but stopped and stood her ground. "Shit, Gordy, you scared me. I thought you were someone else. I was hoping I'd see you, actually. You're not gonna believe it."

He examined her face for truth. He could see her wheels turning behind the mask she wore. And that's just what it was, he realized—a mask. No. There was an explanation. There had to be.

"There was a mix-up with the bus," she said. "The next one to Kentucky isn't until *next* week." She rolled her eyes. "Crazy, huh?"

"Crazy," he agreed.

The door to her motel room swung open and Damien was striding toward them, shirtless and heated, the shadows of his ribs like smears of ash in the gray daylight.

"Well if it ain't the punk who goes around tryna save people," Damien said as he approached. He was amped up on something. He looked at Haley. "Get back to the room."

She looked guilty, caught in something she hadn't prepared for, then hurried back to motel.

Damien leaned down to Gordon's level and peered through the passenger window. "Let me ask you something, motherfucker," he said. "That bitch right there look like she wants saving?" They both looked at Haley as she stood in the doorway watching them.

Gordon tried, but he couldn't read her. "I just want my money back," he said. "That's all."

"*Your* money?" Damien said. "Motherfucker, you ain't got no money. You gave it away, tryna be Super-man. And it was just too easy." He laughed at Gordon and backed away from the car. "And before you go thinking something wild, Superman, like calling the cops or some shit, ask yourself what you think they gonna do. You got nothing but your word, and in this world that don't mean shit with no proof."

He sat there behind the wheel, stunned as Damien strolled away. He felt like the biggest fool, like every low thing his mother had ever told him he was. Twice now he'd played the fool, it seemed. He tried again to convince himself that it had all been Damien's idea, that Haley never would have betrayed him like this. She was a good person, just sick. He'd put her up to it. That was it. She'd mentioned his offer, and Damien had devised the entire scheme. But what was it she had said before? *People do what people do, and I don't do shit I don't want to.*

But she wasn't in her right mind, he told himself, *remember?*

She played you. They both did. And you walked right into it.

He shook his head, but the more he denied what he knew to be true, the deeper the cracks ran into the picture he'd constructed of her, and of his own role in her story.

He turned the cab around, aimed it for the street, not knowing what else to do but drive. Before he pulled out of the parking lot, he checked his side view. There at the door to the room, Damien scooped her up and spun her. He kissed her and squeezed her ass, and they began to laugh.

◇◇◇◇◇

He couldn't call it a plan, not exactly. That would imply too much forethought. But he'd gone home and had two shots of bourbon, then a third, a fourth, and the idea had taken shape with all the detail of a wriggling fish in muddy water. And all he knew now was that he was here.

"Boy, you got some balls, dude," Damien said when he opened the door. He squared up right away, ready to scrap. And though Gordon had plenty of weight on him, he was no fighter, and Damien was a springy little guy who was clearly shy a few screws.

Gordon held up the bottle of 80mg Oxycontin like an offering. Damien's eyes, which had been half-lidded in spite of his apparent energy, widened. "I just want to talk," Gordon said. He looked past Damien at Haley, who was unconscious on the bed, slouched on a mound of dirty pillows in ripped blue jeans and a black bra. This was to Gordon's advantage. "I want to buy her from you," he added. The phrase almost made him wince, as if she was a piece of property to be bought and sold, but he didn't know how else to say it.

"You fucking crazy?" Damien said. "Who do you think I am?"

"Pills and money," Gordon said. "Just let her come with me. She doesn't deserve this."

"And what would you know about what she deserves, Superman?"

He snatched the pills from Gordon before he could reply and stepped aside. Gordon took this as a sign to come in. Damien shut the door and popped the bottle. He looked inside, nodded slowly, and replaced the lid.

"They're yours," Gordon said.

"How much?" Damien said.

"All of them."

"No, the money," he said. "What you gonna pay?" Gordon reached into his pocket, pulled out a fold of bills, and handed it to him. Five hundred dollars he kept at home for emergencies. Damien counted it. "Man, this ain't but a day's work," he said.

"I can get more. Tomorrow. I'm good for it. Just let me take her. Please."

After a moment of staring Gordon down, Damien said, "Yeah, sure, all right, Superman. Go on and fly."

Without thinking, Gordon moved toward Haley, picked up a hooded sweatshirt from the back of a chair and bent down to cover her with it. There was a charred spoon with an array of other paraphernalia on the nightstand, and she had a cigarette, burned clear down to the filter still between her fingers. He was about to pick her up and carry her out when Damien said, "Damn, you really are a stupid moth-erfucker," and Gordon saw his shadow move on the wall as he came up behind him.

Gordon had envisioned some version of this going down, which is why he was able to turn in time, hit Damien with the stun-gun right in the armpit before he could break the beer bottle over Gordon's head. There was a crack and a sizzle, and Damien seized. He dropped to the floor, still clutching the Oxy bottle in one hand. Gordon hit him again and removed the two syringes from his right jacket pocket, leaving the one he'd prepared for Haley in his left. He checked on her. She stirred and moaned but didn't come to. Whatever she'd taken, it had been a lot. In the whirl of his head, he'd anticipated her being awake, maybe having to stun her, too, stick her with enough of the Oxy he'd dissolved to knock her out and hopefully not kill her while he dealt with Damien. He hadn't thought much past that point, though. Once the idea of trying to barter for her had entered his mind, he'd been mostly on autopilot. In fact, he'd scarcely been aware he was following through with it until he was knocking on the door to their room, stomach doing flips, heart stuttering in his chest. But fate, or luck, or some force beyond his comprehension had seen fit to work in his favor. The hard part was over, he thought, removing the needle caps and plugging one into each side of Damien's scraggly neck. He thumbed the plungers, and watched with numb fascination as Damien first convulsed, then began to froth and bleed. The rat poison doing its work. Gordon had seen the aftermath of what the stuff could do plenty of times, but a rodent of this size, up close and personal? It was a sight to behold. Gruesome. Nothing he could have braced himself for.

When Damien finally stopped twitching a few minutes later, red and milky ooze leaking from the various holes in his head, Gordon walked over to the wastebasket and vomited. One quick, burning heave. After that, he felt much better.

He retrieved the money and the pills. He tied up the trash to dispose of later. Through it all, Haley slept.

◇◇◇◇◇◇

There was a pounding coming from upstairs. When her eyes finally opened, it took her a minute to focus and take in her surroundings, which were new to her. Then she began to scream and struggle against the restraints binding her to the armchair. He tried to get her to quiet down, but when she wouldn't, he placed a strip of duct tape over her mouth. He hadn't wanted it to come to this, but had suspected she wouldn't understand, not yet. It would take a little time before she came to her senses. And once she had? No—he wouldn't think about that just yet. Best to handle one thing at a time.

"It's all right now," he said, and shushed her, brushing one of her platinum strands from her face. "Everything's going to be okay this time. Are you comfortable enough?"

He thought she looked terrified, naturally. Of course, the situation was not ideal. But she would come to see this was for the best. He only needed her to calm down so he could explain.

"I knew it couldn't have been you," he said. "No, I knew it had to have been him." She continued to struggle and mumbled something. "Oh, you don't have to worry about him anymore," he said. "They'll find him in the room. It was a mixture. I gave him a lot, wasn't sure how much was enough, you know? I'm a bit new to these things. But I knew you'd never be free if someone didn't do something."

He zoned out for a moment, remembering Damien's choked and spasming body on the motel room floor, the hemorrhaging eyes. The horror of it turned his stomach again and sent a shudder up his spine. But her movements brought his attention back.

Understanding crept into her pale eyes. She strained harder against the bonds and screamed behind the tape with renewed intensity.

"I'll need you to be reasonable," he said.

There was more pounding from upstairs, and he raised his eyes to the ceiling. It was time for his mother's insulin. "That's just Ma," he said. "But don't worry, she'll quiet down soon."

Haley continued to scream and thrash.

"Hey, you like movies, right?" he said, and grabbed the remote from the top of the TV. "Me too." He started the DVD that was already in the player. It was one of his favorites, after all. Maybe it would be one of hers, too, in time. Maybe she'd even

realize she'd been wrong about happy endings. Yes, he thought. She screamed and screamed but soon grew tired. "That's better," he said. He bent down and kissed her on the top of the head, then pulled up a chair and sat down beside her.

◇◇◇◇◇◇

Beach Body
C.A. Rowland

◇◇◇◇◇◇

The seagulls. They landed near the surf every morning and evening. Anne had thought it was to feed, but they sat so still, as if watching, waiting for some signal, when they were to all take off again. As if they knew when it was the right time to leave the sandy area behind.

If not disturbed, the birds sat for at least thirty minutes. Anne wondered if they were just tired of flying and this was a moment of quiet for them. Or perhaps, they too were calmed by the crashing waves of blue-capped in white that raced to meet the light tan sand on Amelia Island, Florida. She hated raw fish and the slimy taste on her tongue but giggled at the thought of birds gathered to have sushi for breakfast.

She breathed in the salty air, feeling it fill her with the lightness of something so fresh and untouched.

She and James walked almost every morning since they'd moved here two years ago. Rain. Sleet. Sunshine. Only the outer coverings changed. This morning was clear and sunny for late December. A light windbreaker and sweatshirt underneath. Together with thick jogging pants, socks, and tennis shoes, the ensemble was more than enough to protect Anne against the elements.

A heavy rain with thunder and lightning, coupled with wind, had hit with a vengeance in the late-night hours the evening before. The sand was littered with bits of shells, seaweed and other debris brought in by the wind and surge of the tides.

James had worn his regular blue jeans, tennis shoes and a flannel shirt. The man never seemed to get cold. They could be in two feet of snow in Chicago, Illinois, as they had been last year, and he'd have on the same outfit. She wondered how it was men could dress in the same thing every day and be happy, when women constantly needed something new or different.

Anne looked down as James squeezed her hand, the cool breeze slipping between them, almost as if he knew she was thinking about him.

They were a picture of contrasts she knew. She, just over five feet tall, slender, fair with blond hair and freckles. James, with dark hair, eyes and broad shoulders that marked him as a man of strength that worked out regularly. His hand, tanned and leathered one from skiing, hiking and running their construction company. Her hand, a few shades of tan paler and softer, encased in light gloves.

Nearing the birds, Anne angled up the beach onto the rougher, drier area. It was this way each morning, her trying to leave the birds in peace. James walking, unaware he might be disturbing any other creature. She'd pointed it out a few times. James had simply said, "That's the nature of their lives. If not us, something else will send them soaring."

Secretly, Anne thought he just liked watching the birds take off. Or dive for fish. James loved hunting and fishing, although it was the hunt and skill rather than the killing of anything. He rarely came home with anything to show for his day in the wild. But always with stories of what he'd seen, or caught and released.

As Anne searched the beach for signs of over-night changes, she focused on a lump of sand ahead. Or at least that was what it looked like until she got a bit closer.

Black peeked through, like a rock or a tarp. Maybe hiding something underneath.

"That's new," Anne said, pointing ahead. "Want to see what it is?"

James turned towards the mound. These side excursions were frequent, and he seemed happy enough to follow Anne's lead on these daily walks.

However, as they got closer, he halted and pulled her back. "Let me check this out first. I don't like the looks of this."

Anne turned to face him. "Do you think some-thing's hurt or died? Like a seal?

"I don't know. Let me check it out first."

Anne watched James looked around and picked up a twelve-inch-long piece of driftwood. He approached the lump, covered by what appeared to be a black tarp and sand. Using the stick, he pulled back a small part, exposing a shoe . . . connected to a leg with what looked like a butterfly tattoo.

Anne sucked in her breath, having moved closer but behind him.

"I told you to stay back." James turned to look up at her with such anger that she took a step back. He pulled his ever-ready cellphone out of his pocket and dialed 911.

◇◇◇◇◇

Anne was still shivering when the police arrived. Not that she was cold, but from the body and James' attitude. She focused on what the officer was asking. The two cops were from the local town, one tall and blond, looking like he should be a lifeguard with trendy sunglasses, and the other almost as tall but thin, wiry with brown hair and a perpetual frown.

"No, we just happened to be walking by," she said in answer to the black-haired cop's question as to how they had discovered the body. "We go one way or the other every morning. Usually starting at the same spot."

"We may have a few more questions," the cop said as he moved off.

Anne turned her head, searching for James, only to find him staring at her. She shivered as it hit her.

James knew the dead woman. At least she assumed it was a dead woman from the shape of her slender calf and the pink and white tennis shoe-- too big for a child or even most teenagers.

She knew she was right. Another of his dalliances. Except this one was now dead. And from what she knew of his latest affair, this was not her.

The police had uncovered the body enough for her to see that this one had blonde hair. James' latest was a brunette.

How long would it take the police to connect the woman to him? Another scandal. No matter if he did anything wrong or not. The shame of another humiliation had landed at her feet. And with that, they'd learn about the current affair. Double the trouble this time.

Anne wasn't sure if her marriage with him or her reputation could survive another Chicago. Sure, he'd retired from his prestigious job with plans for them to travel and live for years.

But the truth was he was forced out–sexual harassment at the office with a subordinate little tramp who was hurt when he moved on. A minor blip in the news but one that all her friends and societal connections had heard and no doubt continued to laugh and gossip about behind her back. These events happened in the best of families, but most had the decency and ability to do it without getting caught or shamed in public. Or there being evidence shoved in the face of their friends and colleagues.

Not to mention their family. Her mother had lived through her father's womanizing and survived without a blemish on the family. Anne had realized that she might have to do the same when she married James but had thought he could be discreet. She'd been wrong.

Mortified in Chicago. Leaving and starting a new life further south had seemed the sensible solution. She still wondered how the young woman had not seen that James would never abandon his wife. It was beyond Anne. James loved the prestige of his job, but he loved the money Anne had inherited more. It gave him a lifestyle he craved and Anne the husband that lent her a different kind of respectability, at least in her circles.

His little escapades? A rebellion that left him feeling in charge with the balance of power in his court.

A dead mistress though was quite another thing.

"You can go," Anne heard the officer say to James.

James caught her hand in his and pulled her back down the beach, toward where they had parked their car. Neither of them saying a word.

◇◇◇◇◇◇

The knock Anne had been expecting came two days later. Anne had found the cottage. Located a bit back from the beach so they didn't have to deal with the summer crowds but close enough to a parking area so that they had access within five minutes of their house.

The cottage had three small bedrooms, one with blue walls and nautical figures, one with a green underwater theme, and one with muted yellow sunny tones. A living room with flowery upholstered furniture against the sandy walls and a kitchen overlooking the tiny backyard. All came with the house, which was fine with Anne. Windows in every room let in lots of light, and breezy curtains floated in the wind.

Anne had opted for what her friends would call a beach rental, leaving her furniture and memories in storage in Chicago, just in case they ever decided to return to the north.

This new place was easy to care for and meant their financial needs were smaller. While Anne had a trust fund, she wanted those funds for travel and vacations. They used James' retirement package for everyday costs. The downsizing allowed them to eat out often although James hated the loss of the two-story walk up they had shared in their toney Chicago neighborhood. While the new start wasn't exactly how either of them had planned to live out their days, it was a beginning.

Answering the door, Anne found the same officers were back, asking for James. Invited in, they sat drinking a cup of coffee, the aroma melding with the fresh sea air that wandered inland, while they peppered him with new questions.

"Mr. Rochester, we've identified the body you found as Charlotte Davis." The blond officer that had taken the lead paused and getting no response, continued. "You told us you didn't know the deceased, but that's not quite true, is it?"

"Officers, I saw the bottom of a leg with a tennis shoe on it. That's not enough to identify anyone," James said.

"But you recognized the tattoo, right?"

"I didn't want to guess. That tattoo seems very common and likely on any number of women's ankles, here and everywhere. But to answer you, yes, I knew Charlotte."

"And what was your relationship to her?" the blond cop asked.

"Anne, why don't I handle these questions alone," James said.

Both officers' eyes turned to Anne. She sat for a moment and then said, "I think I'd rather stay."

James hung his head for a few seconds and then raised it to face the blond officer. "We had a sexual relationship for two months." Turning to Anne, he said, "But it's been over for months."

"And did the sex between you and Miss Davis ever involve erotic asphyxiation?"

"What? No. What are you talking about?"

"Ms. Davis was strangled."

Anne watched James turn pale.

The bond officer turned to Anne. "And did you know about the affair?"

Anne stared at him. "My husband's sexual needs are, shall we say, more than I care to provide. I am aware that he has had a number of affairs over the years. We have no secrets. And when we moved here, I assumed that would continue."

"And what exactly are those needs as you understand them?" the officer asked.

"My husband has a high sex drive. He'd have sex six times a day if I were willing. I'm not. However, if you are asking me if he's ever indicated he would like to try the erotic act—my answer is no."

"So, Mr. Rochester, where were you the night before you and your wife discovered the body on the beach?"

"I was home, here with my wife. Tell them, Anne."

"Is that true, Mrs. Rochester?"

Anne reddened. "As far as I know. Our sleeping preferences over the years have left us sleeping in different rooms. Snoring, his needs. I'd rather not elaborate if you don't mind. And it is personal and would be embarrassing if this was made public."

The officer nodded. "So Mr. Rochester could have slipped out while you were sleeping."

"I don't know about that. I am a very light sleeper and almost always wake up when James is stirring around the house. I feel certain I would have heard him leave ... if he did."

"And what about you, Mrs. Rochester? Where were you?"

"I was here with my husband, but as I said, I was in my bedroom from about ten o'clock until we got up to walk. There were some heavy storms that woke me about one or so, but I got up for a drink of water, then back to bed."

"And did you know Miss Davis?"

"How would I know her? She was not in my social circle," Anne said.

"Okay. I'll ask that neither of you leaves town. We may need to ask you a few more questions."

James was still not speaking to Anne two days later when the police arrived. Why hadn't she simply said he was home with her all night? Didn't she know that it made him a suspect? Or worse, was this her payback for Chicago? And why hadn't they asked if he had heard her leave? Surely they could see she had a motive as well?

James didn't seem to understand that the police were going to discover his history in Chicago. And they would then know that she was already the humiliated wife. If they talked to any of her friends, they'd gleefully report on their bedroom situation. Just as she would on them. Right or wrong, it was just the reality of how things worked in her world.

James had stormed out, only to return later in the day. Angry and unwilling to speak to her, just as she'd done when he'd betrayed her. All would blow over. Always did. In many ways, they were the perfect symbiotic pair.

The knock at the door was not unexpected.

This time the cops arrested James on the spot. Anne tried to ask what had changed, but they simply said they were taking him in and something about new evidence. James demanded she called a lawyer. She said she would.

◇◇◇◇◇◇

Two days later, Anne sat in the office of Peter Keppler, a local attorney, with graying hair, an easy smile and a laid-back attitude that included leaving his plaid shirt unbuttoned. His office was modest as lawyers go. Comfortable chairs and a secretary/receptionist behind a pony wall. Located in an area of town outside of the tourist district, inside an older home, converted into offices.

Peter shared the house with three other lawyers. A large wood desk sat in the middle of the room, and two bookshelves filled with files of what she guessed were open cases dominated one wall. Pictures of old Myrtle Beach clustered on another. She expected a lawyer's office to reek of old wood and lawbooks, but here, it was a mix of lemon Pledge and seawater.

She'd turned to someone who knew everyone in town rather than a big city lawyer. Her reasoning was that a local might have better access and ability within the system. She still wasn't sure if that was the right decision but it had made sense.

Anne listened as Peter outlined the case against James.

"It seems they have found some hairs on the victim that match your husband's. DNA is allowable in court, and they seem to have a very strong case." Peter had paused and Anne had let that sink in. "How long ago did James stop seeing the victim? Do you know?"

"I have no idea. I knew James had moved on to someone new. But the timing is not something I try to watch for. We have an arrangement. He doesn't embarrass me, and I don't ask," Anne said.

"Got it. And about Chicago. Were they any threats of blackmail or anything like that?"

"No. Only the discrimination charge that we've already talked about."

"And here? Did anyone threaten James that you know of?"

"I don't know of anything like that, but you'd have to ask him. He and I never discussed his sexual partners and what they said. Can you tell me if that ever happened? Or could it have happened with the young woman who died?"

"All I can say is that he doesn't understand what is happening or why. I may be able to argue that the hair was on her clothing due to the fact that James had been with her a few months before but that's not a lot. It would help him if you could confirm that he was home that night."

"I'm sorry, but as you know, we sleep in separate beds. With the storm, it took me a while to get to sleep, and I'm sure I slept soundly because I was tired. I know he was there when I went to bed and when I woke up."

Peter sighed and laid his pen down on the yellow pad he'd taken notes on. "All right. That's it for now. I'll need to talk to you again but for now, let's leave it at that."

◇◇◇◇◇

Anne straightened and laid a hand on her back to massage the ache from lifting boxes and packing. She grabbed the tape and closed the lid, securing it before she marked it for contents.

"This is the last one," she said to the strapping young man with the muscular arms.

"Yes, ma'am. We'll lock up the truck and be on our way. I just need you to sign here and initial in three places," he said as Anne wielded the pen.

After the truck left, Anne locked the door, leaving the key under the mat for her real estate broker, Sherry. The closing would be finalized in the morning, and Anne had already signed the papers in escrow. What she wanted now was one last walk on the beach before she headed back to Chicago.

At the parking lot, she parked and locked the car. Then ventured down to the sand, turning in the same direction she and James had turned that fateful morning.

Everything was really as it should be. Charlotte the tramp was dead. Anne still didn't understand how Charlotte could have thought she'd leave James for her. Anne had only wanted to experience what James had, maybe come to comprehend what the draw was. It wasn't like Anne was a lesbian or anything, just curious.

But Charlotte had wanted more. And had threat-ened to tell James. Most likely she had threatened James too, but James would have told her Anne knew and it didn't matter.

Telling James about Anne was another matter altogether. Anne could never let him have that kind of power over her, especially after Chicago.

Anne stared down at the area where she'd dropped the body. Really, the storm had been a godsend. Washing away the tracks of the wheel-barrow she'd used after she'd strangled Charlotte.

Anne had stayed for the trial as the dutiful wife, as she was expected to be, just as she'd given their marriage a new start here. Her Chicago friends were sympathetic and supportive. They encouraged her to return when James was sentenced after two years of waiting for a trial date.

She's argued that she needed to stay while his case was appealed but they'd argued that she could do that from Illinois. And after just the right number of months of discussion, she'd agreed.

Smiling, Anne watched the birds flying, headed off in a new direction. She'd been discreet where James hadn't, both in Chicago and at the beach.

That was really the issue.

The birds certainly understood there was a time for standing still, waiting, and a time to leave. So did she.

Anne turned and walked back to the car.

◇◇◇◇◇◇

Viking Funeral

Nick Kolakowski

◇◇◇◇◇

When they reached Piosa's old property it was nine-fifteen and the sun burned down hard from a crystal-sharp winter sky. Their two cars turned onto a dirt track marked by a thick oak with a sun-bleached yellow ribbon garroting its trunk, and they bumped along until they reached a thinning patch of trees with a white doublewide in the middle of it. The trailer roof sprouted satellite dishes like alien mushrooms. From a window dangled a fading black flag with the skull-and-crossbones above the words 'Sic Semper Deadbeats' in gothic script.

In the lead car, Miller honked. The trailer door creaked open to reveal a teenager long and pale as a remora. He stood blinking in the sunlight and scratched a pimply shoulder and said, "Right-O."

The cars stopped. Alex emerged from the rear one, squinting. Before climbing out, Miller yelled through his open window: "We're here for your brother."

The kid nodded and disappeared inside the trailer. Through the open door they could hear nervous-quick guitar and a gravelly voice singing about hell and damnation. The song reminding Miller of his childhood in Tennessee, the clapboard walls of those back-woods churches quivering as the Sunday congregation inside burst with the love and fury they kept bottled for the week's other six days and twenty-three hours. His brother in the pew next to him, mouthing profane variations on the hymns as he made playing cards appear, disappear, appear from his lapels, sleeves, ears, mouth. As if from a distance he heard Alex say, "What's with the country crap?"

Miller snorted. "That's not country. That's Johnny Cash."

"Cash is country."

"Johnny Cash is Johnny Cash." Miller forced a cheerful note into his voice. "Accept no substitutes." Opening the trunk of his car he set the sloshing gas-cans onto the ground, then opened the emergency kit beside the spare wheel. Stuffed three roadway flares into the back pocket of his jeans.

"Country," Alex said, leaning forward to spit, and nearly tumbled to the frozen ground. He was still drunk from last night. Miller struggled to find a little pity.

The kid reappeared, holding aloft a cardboard box in the manner of a holy offering. For a delirious moment it seemed like he might yodel forth some Latin. Arms raised, Miller stepped forward to receive the relic, concentrating on holding it perfectly level as he moved away. He feared letting the box shift to one side, and hearing the dusty slither from within.

"Oh man," Alex moaned. "You put him in that?"

"Sold the urn online," the kid said. "Paid part of the rent. Not like he'd care."

"We care." Miller wondered what sort of human being would buy a used urn. "That's sort of the point. Alex, grab the gas."

"The Beast's around the back," the kid said. "Don't take this as an insult? But I'll be inside. I deal with grief my own way." He disappeared into the cool dark of the trailer, and Johnny Cash switched to Axl Rose wailing about Chinese Democracy.

Alex hoisted the two gas cans, groaning like it was an epic feat. They circled around the trailer and as their feet crushed the brown grass it shimmered, alive with panicked insects fleeing their advance. The land behind the trailer rose into a low hill dotted with bare elms, and there they found the Mustang.

The car gleamed like a work of art. They had seen it before; Piosa, now residing in the box in Miller's hands, had photographed every stage of its rebirth from rust-heap to cherry. Piosa, who had taken a sniper's bullet above the left eye in the Korengal Valley, dead before the rest of them even heard the shot, dead two years ago today.

Miller set the cremains on the ground and stood. A fast wind rose and rattled the trees. Snow's coming, Miller thought as took one of the cans from Alex's hand, twisted off the cap and doused the Mustang's hood. The gas flowed across the metal and rained softly on the grass. Alex took his cue and used the other can to soak the roof and trunk. Miller opened the passenger-side door and splashed the vintage leather and dashboard with the last of his can and went to retrieve the box.

Alex spun and tossed his cans away, reeled back, almost fell. "Not the best idea, drinking before something like this," Miller told him.

"Don't blame me," Alex said. "The only kid on the block whose daddy got him a case of Bud for Christmas."

"Funny." Miller slid the box onto the driver's seat of the Mustang, noting the keys in the ignition. As if waiting for Piosa to clamber inside, loose one of his patented war-whoops and punch the gas. The smell of fuel in the enclosed space wrung tears from his eyes. "Anything to say for the dear departed?"

Alex clasped his hands and bowed his head. "Piosa. Good man, good operator. Went from us too soon. That's it."

Miller pulled one of the road flares from his cargo pants and took five steps backward from the open car door. "Fire in the hole." The flare burst sparkly-red, reminding Miller of the ones they used to let the Chinooks overhead know the landing-zone was hot. He tossed it in.

The seats caught fire. The flames leapt. They danced. They strutted their stuff across the seats. The windows and dashboard dials burst in applause. The paint crackled in laughter. In seconds a plume of greasy smoke billowed out the open door, scrambling for the sky. The box in the driver's seat blackened and folded in upon itself and its lid curled open and white ash swirled into the hot slipstream and disappeared forever.

Miller and Alex knew the physics of the situation. They retreated twenty yards and hit the dirt and covered their heads in their hands.

With an eardrum-shattering boom the gas tank exploded and a lovingly restored chunk of engine howled into the sky. Heat crisped the hairs on their forearms. After that the Mustang settled into a more peaceful burning.

They stood, Alex saying, "Tell me: Why did Viking funerals ever go out of style?"

From down the hill, the trailer's screen door banged open. The kid on the lawn yelling words lost in the roar of flames. Then he raised a middle finger high and stomped back inside.

Miller felt his mind slip into war mode. He walked toward the burning Mustang, Alex shouting behind him, the questioning sounds of a dog left alone in an unfamiliar place. Miller stopped behind the car and slammed his heel into the rear bumper as hard as he could. The Mustang began to almost imperceptibly creep forward, and gravity saw its chance. Standing on a thrumming left leg Miller offered the whole scene a proper military salute as the car bounced and jostled its way downhill, trailing a party of flames.

Piosa's pride and joy collided with the trailer dead center and the impact knocked the windows out of their frames and the satellite dishes from the roof. The fire spied new territory to conquer and leapt shimmering to the cheap white siding. The whole structure was half aflame before the kid ran out squawking and stood in the yard with his fingers clenched in his hair. Alex and Miller watched everything burn with clinicians' eyes.

"You're losing it," Alex told him, almost as an aside. "Really, truly losing it."

Miller had nothing to say to that. The fire burst from the trailer roof and flapped its orange hands in the sunlight.

"You believe in the concept of blowback?" Alex said. "After everything that happened over there. Ever think someone will come at you for the shit you did?"

Hours later, Miller would blame what happened next on his mind in war-mode, where everything was a threat, and no insult too small for repayment. Quick as a rattler he slammed his right foot into the back of Alex's left kneecap, sending him to the grass. Before the man could suck in more than half a breath Miller had dropped a knee onto his sternum. "Shut up," Miller said.

"You're a total wacko." Alex wheezed, hissing steam. "It's being noticed. Not in a friendly way. People ready to do something about it."

"People got nothing to worry about," Miller said.

Alex rocketed a sloppy fist at Miller's head. Miller slap-pushed his arm aside and followed through with two hits to Alex's jaw and left eye-socket. The violence had been automatic as a sneeze but in its wake Miller felt a little sick. He stared at the bright blood bubbling along the crest of Alex's eye and thought: This is what I do.

"Like they'll take your word," Alex coughed bloody.

"They'll have to. I'm done with this crap." Miller eased upright. The cans had tumbled on their sides, leaking pungent gas. Miller retrieved them and followed the swath of scorched grass to the bottom of the hill, where Piosa's brother knelt at the edge of the burning trailer, warbling into a phone. For an instant Miller considered snatching the device away and tossing it underhand into the fire. Instead he hurled the gas cans into the back of his car and drove away. The pillar of smoke stained his rear-view mirror for two miles before it was lost in hills and distance.

◇◇◇◇◇◇

Long Drive Home

Andrew Welsh-Huggins

◇◇◇◇◇

Shayne made him pick up the tab at the diner they stopped at south of Charlotte, which was when Marty finally realized how much trouble he was in. Normally, Shayne fronted everything with a roll of cash as thick as the business end of a baseball bat, handing it to Marty with a wink right before Marty headed out, which was Shayne's way of letting him know he had him covered, but also that he was good at counting bills. Marty always nodded and said thanks and made a production of pocketing the money with the care of someone in an old war movie receiving orders before heading across enemy lines. Because Shayne had it figured down to the dime— besides the cost of the product, how much Marty and them would need for gas, food and tolls from Columbus to West Palm Beach and back, plus two nights in the Oceanside at $49.99 a night, including cable. Forget about a hotel on the road. That wasn't happening. There were three of them. They could just switch drivers.

Only not this time. This trip it was just Shayne and Marty. Marty didn't know a thing about it until he showed up that night, sitting in the parking lot outside Shayne's apartment, engine running, staying inside the van to keep warm because at thirty degrees the temperature was below normal for November. He didn't want to make the trip—he never really wanted to go—but at least it would be warmer down south. He worried about his sister when he was away. Her and the twins. He worried about them all the time, to be truthful. But especially when he was gone.

"Let's do this," Shayne said, climbing into the van, Mountain Dew in hand. He tossed a backpack in the rear.

"Where's Frankie? And Mike?"

"They're not coming."

"They're not?"

"What I said. Just you and me, partner."

"Why aren't they coming?"

"I told 'em not to."

"Why?"

"Figured just you and me this time. Road trip buddies. Plus I need a vacation. Get some Florida titty for a change. Pinch me some southern fruit." He opened and closed his thumbs and pointer fingers like crab claws. "This Ohio titty's starting to suck. Ha—you get that?"

"But Frankie and Mike always—"

"Frankie and Mike always come because I tell 'em to. This time I'm telling 'em not to. Simple as that. Let's go. One stop and we're outta here."

"What stop?"

"Enough with the questions. Just drive where I tell you."

Marty followed Shayne's instructions, not that he couldn't guess where they were going. What was more important was figuring out was why it was just him and Shayne. Shayne never went with. Shayne gave him the cash and then him and Frankie and Mike spent a day driving and two days buying pills and another day driving back. He handed Shayne the pills and Shayne handed him his cut, and Marty handed half to Janney. His sister needed it a hell of a lot more than he did. And he wasn't going to see her back . . . where she'd been. He promised himself that. Except—

Except the half just wasn't enough.

They found the girl sitting on a porch a block off Sullivant. Thin as a discount store rake with torn jeans and a hoodie the color of winter mud. Her flat eyes said old woman; her face and body said late teens, tops. Shayne opened the back door and she got in and Shayne told Marty to drive around the corner and down an alley.

"You mind?" Shayne said when they stopped.

"Mind?"

"Little privacy?"

So Marty hopped out and stood a discrete distance away and smoked and tried not to listen to the sounds coming from the van. He winced when he heard the girl cry out in pain. He stood another minute and then the door opened and Shayne called him back. He stubbed out the cigarette and returned to the driver's side and drove back around the corner and dropped the girl off.

"Pinched her titties," Shayne said, taking a swig of soda. "Makes 'em yell. They like it, you know?"

Marty didn't respond. He drove up the street and found the entrance ramp to I-70 and got them on the road. He was thinking the girls Shayne got with didn't like their titties pinched. He thought of Janney and the twins, and his shock learning she'd been working some of these same streets to make ends meet. Never again, he told her. So far, he'd kept his promise.

Most of all he wondered why Frankie and Mike weren't coming. He had his suspicions, all right. But it wasn't until they pulled into the all-night diner around 4 a.m. and Shayne ordered them plates of eggs and home fries and sausage and pancakes and toast and then when they were done told Marty to pay up while he went to the can, that he allowed himself to acknowledge the truth.

Shayne knew what Marty had been doing. And he was going to make sure it didn't happen again. And if it didn't happen again and Marty didn't get the extra cash, Janney and the twins were up a creek.

◇◇◇◇◇◇

Alex stared at the knife, not sure she was seeing right.

Black handle. Six inches of gleaming blade. Tip as sharp as a gator's tooth. Lying next to the chopping block where Auntie Jodie left it after cutting up all those ribs last night. She was always slicing ribs, the meat thick and fat, and slow cooking them, and sitting at the picnic table outside tearing the flesh off the bones and wiping the sauce off her lips. Never asking Alex if she wanted any. Because Auntie Jodie only ever asked her two questions.

The first: "You ready?" The second: "How much you get?"

The knife. Just sitting there. Not like Auntie Jodie to leave it out.

Alex had grown accustomed to the questions. She'd grown accustomed to a lot of things. The slaps to her face and the cuffs to her ears. The pills she needed to keep her skin from itching and burning. Always feeling hungry. Yeah, a real routine.

What Alex wasn't used to was being alone this long in the trailer's tiny kitchen that smelled of cooked meat and spilled beer with Auntie Jodie gone and a knife sitting by itself next to the chopping block.

TOUGH

She reached out and touched the handle, half expecting it to disappear, like something with a spell on it. Like in a cartoon movie, one with princesses. With a good princess and a bad witch. But nothing happened. Outside Alex heard gulls crying as they circled the Dumpster and the sound of traffic on the highway headed for the Magic Kingdom and someone yelling to someone else to shut the hell up. But inside the trailer it was quiet. Alex hesitated only a moment. She reached out and wrapped her fingers around the knife handle. It felt cool to the touch. She drew it close, lifting the blade to her face and turning it flat until she could see her eyes reflected in the metal. Weary red eyes, smeared with mascara she never seemed able to wash off. She looked at herself for a whole minute. She realized she couldn't remember the last time she'd gazed in a mirror. She lowered her hand and moved back to the table and slipped the knife into the drawstring bag where she kept the power bars and the make-up and the condoms Auntie Jodie gave her each morning.

"You ready?"

Auntie Jodie, barging through the door. Publix bags hanging from each enormous hand. She dropped them on the table in front of Alex and tried to catch her breath.

Alex said, "You talk to the guy?"

"What guy?"

"The guy. About the job."

"Job?"

"Anna. You said you'd talk to him."

"Right. The job." Auntie Jodie pulled ribs and jars of barbecue sauce from the bags. "Yeah, I did, as a matter of fact."

"Really?"

82

"He's interested. He just needs a little more. It's a finder's fee thing."

"How much?"

"Five hundred."

Alex's heart sank. "Five hundred?"

"Not that much. Two, three days tops, right? No big deal."

"The thing is, I was hoping—"

"Hoping what?"

"Hoping maybe I could take a day off."

Alex's head pitched backwards at the impact of the slap.

"A day off?" A wheeze separating each word. "How you gonna get the five hundred if you don't work?"

"Dunno," Alex said, rubbing her face where it stung the most.

Auntie Jodie dropped her off an hour later. The motel set back from the busy four-lane road. A single palm tree with brown-tinged leaves outside the office, like it survived a brushfire, but just barely.

"Got 'em stacked up for you, so don't be dilly-dallying," Auntie Jodie said, tapping at her phone with fingers like sausages. "I'll be around the corner, you need me."

"Five hundred, and I've got the job?"

"Five hundred and you've got the interview. One thing at a time, all right?"

Alex nodded. She stepped back, drawstring bag in hand, watching Auntie Jodie pull away. When she was gone she walked across the parking lot and used the key to let herself into No. 43. She sat on the bed and waited for the first knock of the day.

She looked at her phone.

It was nine o'clock in the morning.

◇◇◇◇◇◇

TOUGH

Shayne finally took the wheel on the other side of Savannah when Marty told him he couldn't hold his eyes open any longer and was afraid they'd have an accident. Even then Shayne wouldn't do it until they found a Parkers where Marty could buy Shayne more Mountain Dew. One of the twenty-ounce jobbers Shayne liked to guzzle in a single go. As if he had no regard for what he was drinking, or how it tasted . . .

◇◇◇◇◇◇

How it tasted. The idea came to Marty as he drifted off to sleep. Because Shayne sure loved his Mountain Dew. It could work, he thought. It just might work . . .

"Let's go."

Marty jerked awake, staring wildly. They were parked at a rest stop. He looked at his phone. He'd slept only an hour, dead to the world the entire time.

"Wha—?"

"C'mon. My turn to sleep."

Marty rubbed his face, cleared his throat, switched places with Shayne and pulled back on the highway.

Six hours later they were in West Palm Beach. The air was hot and heavy and smelled of salt and diesel and fish left in paper bags overnight. They piled into the room at the Oceanside off U.S. 1 and Marty collapsed onto the bed, face down. "I'm gonna grab some chow," Shayne said. "Want anything?"

"I'm good," Marty said. In a minute he'd call Janney. He knew he should call someone else, but he couldn't risk it, with Shayne around. "Grab some chow" Shayne's way of saying, "I'll be right back—don't even think about going anywhere."

Marty could think of nothing else.

Well, that and the Mountain Dew.

◇◇◇◇◇◇

I want 2 b Anna.

◇◇◇◇◇◇

The first thing of substance Alex texted to Auntie Jodie after they traded cell phone numbers. Feeling shy as she did. Because she'd never told her dream to anyone, even her sister. She couldn't say for sure how many times she'd watched Frozen, but a fair estimate might be two hundred viewings. There'd been that stretch over the summer when the temperature in Jacksonville peaked at ninety-five plus for two or three weeks running, and all she'd done was sit next to the window air conditioner and watch the movie over and over until it cooled down just enough to flop on the couch and fall asleep.

Anybody else?

She decided Pocahontas was an OK second choice, especially considering her Gramma was supposed to be one sixteenth or something Seminole. Ariel or Jasmine would be all right too, but not Belle. No way. How could you fall in love with a monster, no matter how nice he was? She explained all this in a flurry of texts to the lady who called herself Auntie Jodie, making sure she understood Anna was her first choice by a long shot. She said she understood. She said her brother knew a guy at Disney who did the casting for the park princesses, and it wouldn't be a problem. That made sense, Alex thought, since Auntie Jodie was the one who'd placed the online ad for "Disney Princess Models" that she answered on one of those hot July days right after her eighteenth birthday. And sent her money for bus fare and new clothes within two days, no questions asked.

Alex thought she'd died and gone to heaven when she saw the hotel room Auntie Jodie put her up in the first couple of days and the meals she treated her to, in restaurants with actual cloth on the tables. Alex was so happy she didn't mind when Auntie Jodie said she had to leave the hotel for a couple of days and stay with her while she scheduled the interviews with the guy. And she felt truly sorry for Auntie Jodie when she arrived home one night and explained, shamefacedly, that the guy was willing to meet with her, but she might have to "play along a little" depending on what happened, because that's how these guys work.

Alex played along, though she hadn't wanted to.

She played along with the next guy, too.

And the next one, and he hurt her badly enough that once she'd stopped crying she accepted the pill to help with the pain that Auntie Jodie offered apologetically as she wiped her own eyes, like marbles pressed into the dough of her face, and put her arm around Alex's shoulder.

And then cuffed her, telling her to be more careful next time.

And then gave her another pill.

That was in September. Now it was November. And she still needed another five hundred before she could get the interview.

"So talk to the guy tomorrow?" Alex said that afternoon.

"He had to cancel," Auntie Jodie said. "Probably Thursday."

"Thursday for sure?"

"Fingers crossed," she wheezed.

Alex tried to zone out when they got back to the trailer, but it was hard to relax with Auntie Jodie stomping around the kitchen, yelling that she couldn't find her knife. Alex just stared at the TV, thinking about Anna and crinkly dresses with puffy sleeves and five hundred dollars.

And the knife. And what she might do with it if Auntie Jodie didn't stop hitting her.

◇◇◇◇◇◇

Even with Shayne along the routine was the same. They started at EveryMed Rx Pharmacy, where Marty presented the forged prescription for Oxycodone and turned over a hundred dollars and received two full bottles and a form to sign saying they were for personal medicinal use only. They went to Family Ready Pharmacy next, repeating the drill, and BetterMed Rx after that. They drove past Walgreens and CVS and Walmart. It wasn't worth the risk. Those places had computer systems now and you had to show your license.

It was late in the afternoon when they arrived at Chronic Care Management Clinic on an access street off the airport road. When it came their turn they presented themselves, explaining they'd hurt their backs at a construction site in Pompano Beach. Marty went in first. The doctor who saw him was pear-shaped, pale-skinned and had thick, brushed-back hair the color of crow feathers shed in a downpour.

"Show me where it hurts." The doctor's eyes soft and sympathetic.

"I think it's my L5, S1," Marty said by rote, reaching around to his lower back. "It's popped before."

"I would concur," the doctor said, not moving from his chair. He wrote a prescription and handed it to Marty and told him he hoped he felt better and said the dispensary was down the hall. Marty nodded, not bothering to explain he knew that already. He

handed over the cash and received four bottles in
return and went outside and waited for Shayne.

"I'm gonna grab some chow," Shayne said, looking
at his watch. "Want anything?"

They ate pizza in the motel room, curtains open
so they could watch the sunset over the ocean, even
being the ocean was almost a mile away. Finished,
Marty leaned back on his pillow, fighting sleep, and
also a feeling of hopelessness. It was around this
time, the work for Shayne done, that normally he
was accustomed to saying so long to Frankie and
Mike and taking a side trip down the road. To a house
that wasn't much more than a shack with a sign
outside advertising herbal drugs and ozone therapy.
A place where he could get double the pills for the
price at the clinic. It had been so easy. On his return,
present Shayne with exactly the number of pills he'd
budgeted for. Then, afterward, take the extra pills
he'd bought, yeah, technically with Shayne's money,
and distribute them on the sly through his buddy, and
take the money from those sales and give it all to
Janney. Between Marty's cut from Shayne and the
side dough she could make rent and buy diapers and
food and not ever go back to the streets. Back to the
pimp and his helper girl who treated Janney so bad.

But not tonight. Tonight Marty lay on the bed
in the motel room while Shayne watched a Survivor
show and drank his Dew and worked his phone. Marty
drifted off, only to awake with a start hours later.
He'd heard a shout—a high-pitched feminine yell.
He looked at the other bed and saw a girl on top of
Shayne trying to keep his hands off her breasts as
Shayne said, "You like that, don't you?"

In the morning Marty woke up and then Shayne
woke up and they did it all over again.

◇◇◇◇◇

"I got to $500 yesterday," Alex said. "I counted it. So how come—"

"How come is the guy's not feeling well and asked if we could meet Monday instead," Auntie Jodie said. "And I told him yeah, because he's being nice enough to meet with me."

"With us."

"What?"

"You said meet with you. But he's meeting with us, right? Because this is for the Anna job I want."

"Right," Auntie Jodie said, hand planted on her sofa-cushion sized chest as she tried to catch her breath. Better on her chest than Alex's face. "Meet with us. That's what I meant. Here's a chance to get a little ahead, is all I'm thinking. Maybe just half a day. Whaddaya think?"

"I think I'd rather meet the guy."

"I'd rather meet the guy too. Monday's only three days."

So Auntie Jodie dropped Alex back at the motel. And noon came, and she stopped by to check on her, and brought her a sandwich and a water bottle, and cuffed her, and apologized between shallow breaths as she explained there was just one more, some tourist, and then they could go home.

"How long," Alex said, resting her hand on the drawstring bag. Feeling the outline of the knife under the material. Sneaking a glance at Auntie Jodie, guessing where the breastbone might be underneath all that fat.

"He's on his way now."

"Then we see the guy Monday?"

"Then we see how the guy's feeling Monday."

"Hope he's feeling better," Alex said.

"On his way," Auntie Jodie said.

◇◇◇◇◇◇

TOUGH

Friday morning they hit EveryMed a second time because Marty knew a different pharmacist came on duty to work a three-day long weekend shift. They planned to visit two other clinics afterward, but the line was so long at the first they lost an hour. Even so, Shayne seemed content when they walked out.

◇◇◇◇◇◇

"We got exactly what I counted on. What I calculated. You've got the routine down, partner. Have to hand it to you. Not a pill more or less. Glad I came along, see how it's done. See where you go. I'm feeling good about this. I may make it a regular thing. I like being on the road. Different sights. Different fruit." He did that crab claw thing again with his fingers.

"So we're heading home?"

"Just one stop on the way. Little east of Orlando. Then it's back to O-HI-O. You homesick already?"

Marty thought about Janney. The panic in her voice when he'd snuck the call to her that morning, while Shayne was in the bathroom. The sound of the twins' crying in the background.

"Just a homebody, I guess."

"Not me. I like to get out and go."

"I'll pack the van."

They drove until Cocoa West and then Shayne told him to exit and read him directions and they drove a few miles more until they came to a light. Marty turned right, and then left, and then into the parking lot of a motel with a single palm tree by the business office with brown-tinged leaves.

"Wait here," Shayne said. "I won't be long."

"OK," Marty said. Trying to keep his voice natural. Waiting until the van door slammed shut and Shayne was walking away to reach down and grab Shayne's soda bottle.

◇◇◇◇◇◇

"Ow!"

"You like that, huh?"

"No—stop it," Alex said.

"How about like this?"

"Ow! That really hurts."

"I like it too," the man said.

Alex arched back, trying to keep him inside her but also lean far enough away that his hands couldn't reach her breasts. When his fingers first touched them she recoiled inside, as she always did, but figured it wouldn't last long because this guy looked and acted like he needed it bad and was in a hurry. Creepy looking, eyes the color of a palmetto bug's back. The sooner he was gone the better. Then he pinched her and she jerked back, yelling at the pain, and instead of apologizing he laughed and did it again.

She couldn't lean back far enough.

"Ow!"

She rolled off him and scooted to the end of the bed.

"The fuck are you doing?"

"I told you that hurts."

"And I told you I like it. Get back up here."

"Not if you're going to do that. That's not the deal."

"The deal?" The guy laughed. "The deal's what I say it is."

"No it ain't," Alex said, fumbling for her panties. "You need to leave."

"I'm not leaving until I get what I paid for."

"I didn't say you could pinch—"

"Listen, bitch—" he said, slithering down the bed.

"No!" she said as he grabbed her left arm. She pulled free and fell to the floor, landing on top of the drawstring bag.

"No?" he said, laughing again as he reached for her.

It was a bit of an operation, it turned out, chewing the pills to a pulp, then carefully drooling them into the bottle of Mountain Dew, one dollop of spit at a time, mouth getting dryer and dryer at each go. Marty had done ten so far, which he figured was enough, but who really knew? Pure speculation that Shayne wouldn't taste the pills as he drank the soda, though one thing in Marty's favor was how thirsty Shayne always was after a girl. What he would do with Shayne later on, if it worked, he hadn't thought about. He'd get to that. Janney might—

He stopped. He stared as a large woman—a very large woman—limped toward the room Shayne disappeared into a few minutes earlier. She walked with difficulty, legs like pile drivers and arms like sofa cushions. Flesh straining to burst from her black t-shirt and sweatpants. She knocked at the door, waited, knocked again, and went inside.

Shit. This wasn't good. Shayne had the keys with him, like he always did. If that woman—

He had to do something. Shayne had the keys. And Shayne had to climb safely back in the van so he could drink his Mountain Dew.

Marty glanced around the parking lot, looked again, got out of the van and walked fast toward the room.

"You stupid, stupid girl," Auntie Jodie said. Wheezing so badly she had to lean against the wall as she took in the scene before her.

◇◇◇◇◇◇

"I didn't mean to," Alex said, head ringing from the blow from Auntie Jodie's fist. She used a fist this time. "He wouldn't stop pinching me."

"Like that matters."

"He hurt me."

"Who cares—"

They both turned at the sound of the room door opening. A man stood in the doorway and stared.

"Holy crap," he said.

◇◇◇◇◇◇

It took a moment for Marty to process everything. Shayne on the bed on his back, a knife jutting from his left eye, blood pooling around him. A half-naked girl crouched at the end of the bed, a welt rising on her left cheek. The enormous woman glaring at him as she took deep, gasping breaths.

"Who—?" he started to ask.

Before he could finish she was coming for him, arms outstretched like giant rolling pins as she lurched in Marty's direction. He braced himself and at the last second punched her soft chest with the palms of both hands and to his surprise she staggered backwards and fell over, the floor shaking a little, and just lay there, struggling for breath. Wheeze. Pause. Wheeze. Pause.

"Who are you?" the girl said.

"Who's that?" Marty replied, pointing at the woman.

"She's—"

"She needs help," Marty said.

"Like him?" the girl said, gesturing at Shayne.

Marty stood there, head spinning. He glanced down and realized he was still holding the bottle of Mountain Dew. He looked at the girl and then at Shayne and then the lady on the floor and then back to the girl. He saw how the girl stared at the lady. He thought of Janney and the twins and the streets he'd pulled his sister off. Away from the girl working for the pimp—not quite as fat as this lady, but getting there—the girl who kept hitting Janney for no reason . . .

"Sure," Marty said. "Like him."

He kneeled, twisted the top off the soda, and used his left hand to gently raise the woman's head. She blinked, confused, but even in her state gratefully took a drink. And another. And another. When the bottle was mostly empty Marty lowered her head just as gently. After a couple of moments she snorted and gasped and her chest rose and fell three times like a hill riding an earthquake. After a couple more moments her head fell to the side and she wasn't wheezing anymore.

Marty said, "Are you all right?"

The girl glanced at Shayne, naked and spread-eagled on the bed with a knife in his eye.

"I guess. Are you?"

Marty looked at the woman on the floor, bubbles of spit on her lips.

"Yeah."

Marty turned his back while the girl gathered her clothes and went into the bathroom. When he heard the door shut and water running he went through Shayne's clothes. He found the keys easily enough. Next he found Shayne's wallet. It held all of eleven dollars. Disgusted, he threw the wallet and Shayne's pants on the floor. The pants landed with an odd thud. Marty picked them up and felt around and reached inside the right pants leg.

The girl came out of the bathroom. She was wearing sneakers and jeans shorts and a t-shirt with a princess and some kind of snowman on it.

"What is that?" she said.

"It's money."

"I can see that. How much?"

"A lot."

"A lot lot?"

He told her that it was.

The wad of cash Marty found in the sewn-in pocket down the leg of Shayne's pants was as thick as the business end of a baseball bat. But unlike the wad Shayne always gave Marty, this wasn't just twenties. These were hundreds. And there was another wad just like it in the other pants leg.

"We should go," Marty said.

"We?"

"You can come if you want."

"Where?"

"I'm from out-of-state. Columbus, Ohio."

"I'm from here. Jacksonville, actually."

Neither of them spoke for a second.

"Could I have some money?" the girl said.

"Money?"

"You said it's a lot."

"How much?"

"I'm not sure." She pulled a pile of greasy bills from a drawstring bag. "I don't have quite enough."

"For what?"

She told him.

Then she said, "Where's that money from?"

He told her.

"So how about it?"

He thought about the twins and Janney and the streets she'd been on.

"It's OK with me as long as we leave right now."

He dropped her off at the Magic Kingdom entrance an hour later. Gave her four bottles of pills and half of Shayne's cash. The remainder was still three times what he normally earned after a trip. More than enough for his sister and the twins. He watched the girl march toward the entrance gates, head held high and drawstring bag over her shoulder like a royal satchel or something, until he couldn't see her anymore. Then he turned around and headed for the highway. He needed to be on his way. It was a long drive home, and it was just him behind the wheel.

◇◇◇◇◇◇

Masonry

Rob McClure Smith

◇◇◇◇◇◇

The late afternoon sky was that blue called sky-blue. A sky so clear and true you could put your fist through it. A plane cut a diagonal swath across it. Cowan wanted to be up there, oblivious to harm.

It was 2.30.

Near the turnstiles at King Street slouched a young man. His hair cut in a fade and topped with a purple do-rag knotted in front, wide-legged Rocawears bunched on a pair of reverse-laced red K-Swiss. He had the look, right down to the old RG3 sweatshirt over a snow-white tee, and he was trying way too hard not to check out the arrivals. A blue knapsack nestled between his feet. It was the knapsack was off.

Cowan took the other exit. He crossed by the Amtrak depot and climbed Shooter's Hill to the Masonic Memorial. Crossing Callahan, he looked back to see a blue bag slung over a shoulder and a phone clamped to an ear.

The Memorial was fashioned after the Light-house of Alexandria. But no Egyptian would have concocted nine floors of Doric, Ionic and Corinthian into this stone tier cake monstrosity. The information board was a dark solemn black. Open daily. No dogs. No filming. Proper attire required. This fucking donkey jacket would be the death of him. On top of the board a golden crest, sun at the top, moon at the bottom, columns at upper left and right surmounted with globes, sheaves of wheat, tools and pomegranates. In the center a "G" surrounded by a square and a compass and '1910.' In crimson three stars and two horizontal stripes. *In Memoriam Perpetuam.*

He chose the curving path on the left, scaling another step tier, then another. Up and up. The embankments framing the steps stippled brown. Landscaping minimal, sparse bushes ranged symmetrically. No cover, a blank and deserted place. One tier from the top, a glass case with reproduction of Brady's 1864 panoramic view. The city of Robert E. Lee was gray and smoky, a military tent village erected where the train station now was, a row of arches, like on a rich man's croquet lawn. Cowan read about the Ellsworth Avengers on a sepia daguerreotype, located landmarks then and now, contemplated the hidden meanings of architecture. Sloping downhill, another stone G in the square and compass. To his right the young man from the Metro. He had followed him and it wasn't for his autograph.

"Aight." The kid tapped a finger on his do-rag, blue-black tat of a spider-web like a bruise on the side of his neck.

They stared at a distant horizon, low rooftops, distant snaking blue, a far away Ferris wheel, unturned. A flag flapped on a flagpole causing it to creak. Cowan saw the butt of a pistol protruding from the waistband of the kid's boxers. He was supposed to.

"What you suppose the big G stands for?" he asked.

The kid stared at Cowan like his question was mined.

"Big G on the stone there?"

"George."

"You think?"

"Uh-huh. George Washington, man, founding father freed the slaves and shit."

"Not God?"

The kid considered this. "Nah."

"Geometry then?"

"Don't give a shit, cuz. Whatev."

"You should," Cowan said, angrily. "Big difference between God and George. God doesn't have a name, so the theologians say. But if he did it wouldn't be George. Who'd take a God called George seriously? 'Come out the burning bush, George, you're scaring the kids!' George doesn't have the right ring to it. Doesn't that bother you any?"

The kid gave Cowan the heavy-lidded look he likely reserved for homeless D.C. crazies. "I ain't got to bother about nuthin' but be black and die, slim."

"What you think his name would be then?"

"God."

"Besides that."

"Fuck is with you man?"

"Seriously If God had a name what'd it be?"

"Sumthin like. . . " The kid pondered his knuckles. "Fuck I know."

"You're not even trying." The silence lasted about seven years.

"Sumthin like Mahabone maybe," the kid spat, finally.

"What?"

"Mahabone. I made it up. Got some serious ji voodoo vibe to it. See, I was God I'd want a serious motherfuckin name scare the shit out folks got me bent." He tilted his chin at the declining sun, content. "Mahabone, hell. I'm a liking that. They be shittin' their pants old Mahabone come round."

"You got a name?"

"You hear me ask yours?" He held Cowan's gaze. Finally, "Yeah. I got a name."

"That's good," Cowan said. "A name's useful. That's how come my cat is called Susan."

The kid unzipped the knapsack. Cowan watched. Instead was extracted a two-thirds full 40-ounce of Country Club. A cap unscrewed. Amber fluid sloshed.

"I see you brought your own urine sample."

"You ever shut the fuck up, man? I'm here appreciatin' the nature and shit."

The kid took a deep swig of the malt and wiped his mouth on his sleeve. He had to hold the bottle with both hands to tip it, like he was playing a brass instrument.

"Did you know beer is made from barley?" Cowan asked. "That gut rot is derived from corn."

The kid screwed the cap back on and adjusted the bottle on the parapet. "Do I look like I give a fuck?"

"That's the only Country Club you'll ever see the inside of." Cowan gestured at the Memorial. "Ever gone inside?"

"I ain't ever been in that joint." The kid grimaced. "Fuck is these creepy pillars and shit?"

A couple, in prosperous middle age, climbed the steps. The kid observed their approach, eyes flitting, evaluating terrain. They passed, on to the entrance, where they paused in an attitude of worship.

"I do like them boxers," Cowan said. "Very pretty. I knew a girl had panties the exact same shade of blue and red and white. I think her name was Wonder Woman. Is that the new concealed-carry underwear I've read about? What you plan to do with the gun? Shoot your balls off?"

The kid tilted his chin at him. "Kill your ass. Do the world a favor."

"Not here though." Cowan said. "All these sight-seers. Look, here's Tiger Woods."

Prince Hall came down the steps backward, snapping a photograph on his phone. He wore a green jacket.

"Tourists don't give no shit. You know how they do. They from Minnesota and such." The young man waxed philosophical. "See no evil, know what I'm sayin'?"

"You all getting acquainted?" Hall joined them. He wore a pair of too-large Locs sunglasses, a Redskins snapback high on his brow. "What's good cuz?" He offered his fist to the kid for a pound and they performed an elaborate ritual handshake.

"Man, I'mma keep it a hunnit, don't like this shit. Naw. Way in the open, know what I'm sayin'? Like the Kennedy Center. Should be in the cut for a deal like this."

"What you got there?" said Hall, gesturing at the bottle. "You can't be doing that here. What the matter with you, Jalil? Get a grip."

"Listen to this motherfucker talk for five and you be drinkin too."

Prince walked behind Cowan to fingerwalk his jacket pockets, hunkering to track with his palms the inside seam of his jeans, socks. He removed his wallet.

"I appreciate you hooking up with us, Mr. Cowan."

"If you're feeling frisky shouldn't you ask me out for a drink first?"

Prince palmed his chest pocket for a cigarette. "Smoke?"

"I'm looking after my health." Cowan grinned. "I'm figuring to live a long time."

Hall laughed, tossing the wallet to Jalil who rifled it.

101

"Next you'll be asking if I want a blindfold."

Hall lit with the flick of a Bic, inhaled deeply. "I'm not with you."

"Before the execution. Like the last cigarette."

Hall blew a streamer of smoke. "That's a morbid thought. I'm going to finish this jack," he said. "Then we're going to stroll back around there admire the fine architecture."

"I'm not going anywhere," Cowan said, reasonably. "Sorry. I like it here. I can appreciate the nature and shit, that right?"

Jalil sniffed. "I think we got a crazy. Talkin' to me about the name of God and some shit." He finished with the wallet, finding nothing of interest, stuffing two twenty dollar bills in his pocket. "We bout done here?"

"This one says the G in the block there is for George," Cowan said. "I say God. Want to be the casting vote, Prince?" Cowan blinked a few times at him. "Prince. What a silly name."

"Giblum." Hall examined the tip of his cigarette like it was a Rorschach, flicked dead ash. "It means stone squarer."

"I'm surprised."

"You get a free education when you serve. You be all you can be, no one tell you that?" He looked in Cowan's eyes. "You'd have been better never come to this city."

The tourists returned and the men exchanged a glance. Hall made a delicate gesture with his hands, an oblique sign.

Cowan looked at the sprawl of city. "You get a good view up here. Where was it you served? Afghanistan? Iraq?"

"You don't want to know where I've been or the things I done."

"Prince," said Cowan, thoughtfully. "Say, you weren't named after the midget in the purple suit? The one sang Darling Nikki?"

Hall narrowed his eyes slightly. "Great song that," was all he said.

The tourists stopped by the emblem. Hall drummed his fingers on the railing.

The sun hung lower in the sky, an invitation to night. They moved away.

"I'm not coming with you," Cowan said, quietly.

"I think it's in your best interest."

"I'm finished either way." Cowan shrugged. "I'm just not up for making it convenient. You'll have to do for me here, like this."

Hall flinched. "It's a hard world. You know that."

Cowan needed to think carefully and act quickly. For now, jabbering like an idiot would have to do.

"Must be hard for you being a professional and here you have to work with amateurs like Lil' Wayne here."

Hall ashed his cigarette on the railing and a slow rain of orange flecks descended. "You have to use what's at hand when you're building," he said, turning a complete 360, seeing no one for miles. "Different tools for different purposes." He flicked his butt on the grass, reached into his jacket pocket, made more significant eye contact with Jalil.

They wouldn't shoot him. They had something else in mind. Something quieter.

"What about this tool?" Cowan asked, edging closer to Jalil. "When this is done, you going to do for him too?"

"What the fuck this crazy rambling 'bout?" Jalil asked.

"Forget to tell you about that?" Cowan tut-tut-ted. "You didn't tell him how royalty cleans up after itself. That's a sin of omission."

"I hate to be rude, but you're starting to bore me." Hall nodded at Jamil, who didn't move. Just stared blankly.

Cowan toe-shuffled closer, within arm's length of the bottle now.

"You need to kill here, cuz," Prince said, discomfited. "This one just trying to syce the situation."

"I been thinking about how that shit went down my own self."

"We talk about this later, aight?"

"Hold up, but way Carlton was buggin'. . ."

Jalil didn't finish because Cowan scooped up the liquor bottle with both hands and brought it down hard as he could on the purple do-rag. There was a dull hollow glassy thud and the cap popped. Blood and liquor sprayed on the stonework. Jalil staggered sideways like a stunned cow and Cowan smacked him on the cheekbone with the bottle so hard it shattered. He was left holding the wide jagged neck. Jalil's knees buckled and his eyes rolled back white, like a man far gone in drink. He toppled onto the embankment, thrashing, his legs kicking as though pedaling an invisible bicycle.

The gun spun between the railings and onto the emblem, clattering on the stone. Cowan was trying to gauge where it went when Prince's body flew into his, a linebacker's hit. The momentum sent them off the parapet and onto the carved square. It was a four foot drop, but they landed hard and awkward on the stone G. Cowan's back spat rapid sparks of pain. Only a tsunami of adrenalin and terror got him upright.

Hall was hurt too, his right shoulder dislocated. His arm hung limp by his side and he had the look of a man who had failed to accomplish a basic task, targeting fury like a laser at his own ineptitude. He eyed Cowan through a mist of hurt and rage.

Cowan scrambled across the stone searching for the missing gun.

With the subtlest flick of his wrist a small ivory knife appeared between Hall's fingers. Cowan backed up across the G as Hall advanced, dabbing the knife at his chest. He felt the indent of the stone letter under his feet. The man was trained to kill hand-to-hand. But he was injured, switching the blade to his left hand. His semi-crippled status evened things up. The third time Hall thrust, wincing as he did so, Cowan skewered his wrist with the bottleneck.

"I'm going to kill you," Hall bared his teeth. He looked at the glass embedded in his wrist, blood spurting around it. He took a step, his face crumpled with pain. "I'm going to kill your ass. Kill your ass," he chanted. But the knife hung limp.

They circled one another on the emblem, in the attitude of dancers. Hall on the compass: Cowan on the square. He expected to be numbed by panic, but this close to death he felt untroubled. How few thousand years ago it was other dancers had stood here, plodding slowly in a darkness of fetid caves, befouling themselves in ceremonies of fear with gestures bloody and offerings bloody given up with knives bloody to some impassive stone idols. He tasted swamp history in his mouth and scented in the wind an ancient, reeking odor and wanted very much to live and was no longer afraid.

When Hall made another lunge, Cowan tugged on the elastic in his sleeve and the plywood with the razor blade embedded in it snapped into his fingers.

He jinked and stroked the blade across the exposed cheek. It slit Hall temple to chin. The skin tore like paper. Hall gave a cry and fell to one knee. Cowan kicked him in the jaw.

The spurting made a red tributary across the indentation of the square and compass. Cowan crept to where Hall lay splayed on the stone. He wasn't moving.

"Prince," he said, holding the razor's edge in front of him.

More red pooled now and the handle protruding from Hall's neck quivered each time a jet squirted under it.

"Isn't nobody killed me yet," Cowan whispered.

The slab was veined with blood.

Cowan found the gun in a bush. He knew fuck-all about guns. He didn't even know how to take the safety off.

Jalil sat up, feeling at his face with his hands. One cheek was badly swollen and an eye closing fast. Cowan jammed the gun in his ear. "I told you drinking was bad for you," he said.

"What the fuck you do?" moaned Jalil, blood seeping between his fingers.

"You've heard the expression 'hitting the bottle'? This time the bottle hit you. I think you might be concussed. That'd be hard to tell with you, son." Cowan tracked the cut on the kid's head with his palm. "You're going to need a doctor but—"

"I don't believe in them," Jalil groaned. "Fucks stick you with needles and shit."

"You need stitches. It won't hurt."

"'It won't hurt' always does," Jalil said, despondent.

Cowan hauled him to his feet and, shoving the gun in his back, forced him to look at the body on the emblem, arms forming a 90 degree angle, like a final signal of distress.

"Head hurts like a motherfucker," Jalil observed.

"That could be you," Cowan said. "Lying there. Just saying."

"Could be. But ain't." Jalil shrugged. "I didn't like him anyways. He had a bad attitude."

The blood made the stone slippery. Cowan had never once considered the slipperiness of blood.

"Take off your jacket," he ordered.

"Nah."

"Give us the fucking jacket."

Jalil handed it to him. Cowan took off his own. "Here," he said, handing it over. "Wipe that stone off with this."

"You serious?"

"Do I look serious?"

"I dunno what you look like."

Jalil scrubbed. The declining sun freakishly seemed to dart its rays to the center. Both of them looked up, disturbed. Then returned to the task at hand.

"Move the body off first," Cowan said. "And be careful you don't slip and fall. That would be embarrassing." He pulled on the sweatshirt. "It's important not to embarrass yourself." He flipped the hood and sat hunched like a monk with the gun still leveled at Jalil. The hoodie made him self-conscious. His back hurt and his legs were shaking again. He wondered if he was going into shock. "Now how's about you drag it under that bush, see it?"

"You goin to shoot me or what?"

"Depends."

Jalil kicked the body into concealment, wiped his hands clean on the grass.

"You know how to make this all go away?" Cowan asked.

"How you mean?"

"I mean can you make a call to your people and make this go away? Like it never happened. You connected? Or is that what Prince did before he abdicated?"

"Maybe."

"Do it. Then go get some stitches."

"I think I got a number some place. You not goin' to shoot me?"

"I want to, but I need the bullets where I'm going."

"The safety is on."

"Yeah, I figured."

"Can't shoot nobody with the safety on. You retarded?"

"You going to make that call or not?"

"What I say?"

"Tell them you fucked up. Tell them the guy you meant to waste got away. Say he ran towards the Metro. Tell them you need a body disposed of."

Jalil's eyes never left the gun as he spoke. Cowan took his phone and threw it against the stone.

"The fuck?"

"The cell phone is destroying the art of conversation."

"That a new iPhone!"

Cowan took off the safety. "Go find my wallet."

Jalil came back with it. "You take bad photos, man. They do the license over you ask. Don't nobody have to go through life looking that ugly-ass."

"Keep the 40 and put it toward a new coat." Cowan stuffed the wallet in his pocket. "Then get yourself a new line of work. You're not cut out for this. Be an exotic male dancer or a postman or something."

"You not goin to shoot me?"

"You keep bringing it up I'm liable to."

Cowan lowered the gun and took off down the steps.

"You really goin to the Metro?" Jalil called after him.

Cowan turned and aimed the gun. "It matter?"

"I ain't say shit." Jalil's lip was in a full pout. "You sure you need to be keeping that jacket?"

"Uh-huh."

He walked along King, glancing nervously at traffic headed east. The street whirled like the blades of a fan. He went into the Austin Grill, famished. Maybe that's what killing someone did. Gave you an appetite. He asked to be sat at a window table, one overlooking the main drag.

4:03, night fast falling, headlights on. He settled back, looked at the rack of glasses by the bar, the longhorns above the kitchen, the array of weird masks on the brick walls. Even that scary-ass Frida Kahlo looked seductive tonight.

The waitress was checking him out. She was young, a leggy sloe-eyed blonde in too-tight jeans and a low-cut blouse. He didn't attract that kind of attention from this young a woman anymore. In his early thirties, a cloak of invisibility had descended on him. Perhaps he had the look of a stone-cold killer tonight: maybe the danger he exuded made him more attractive. Something evolutionary.

She returned with his Pepsi, big-eyeing him. She was staring so blatantly that he felt obligated to stare back. She was pretty as all get-out. When she brought his order, she put on the tray a glass of water without ice and a pile of napkins. She leaned her breasts across him and he deep-whiffed her perfume as she whispered in his ear. "Sir, there's blood. It's on your face." He looked at her. "It's, like, all over your cheeks."

He dipped the napkin and wiped the blood away. There was a lot of it, and it wasn't even his. He depleted the pile.

"I think I must have cut myself," he said.

Her look of concern was tinctured, Cowan realized, with horror.

"There's blood on your hands too," she said.

There was.

◇◇◇◇◇◇

Once Upon a Time in Chicago

Tia J'anae

◇◇◇◇◇◇

A dead silence serenaded Carla's nerves, under the streetlights.

That had never happened before during one of their backseat romps. Arron laughed at her jumpiness, playfully teasing her insecurities to being afraid of the black snake between his legs that couldn't wait to ravage her.

His mischievous smile gave her little comfort.

Carla knew the dank Chicago streets well enough to instinctually sense danger lurking in the shadows. The asphalt and grime were quiet enough to notice; her intuition wouldn't let go the ominous warnings waiting to make their acquaintance without a proper invitation. Ignoring her survival instincts, she compromised the gnawing feeling in her stomach to flee; instead she indulged Arron's insatiable desires.

She knew better than to ignore the voices in her head, but it was a small price to pay for ensuring Arron would spring for the Coach purse she had her eye on at Marshall Fields. Ordinarily, quick blowjobs spread over a couple of weeks would be all the inspiration he needed for a shopping trip. But Carla wanted it tomorrow, before any other boss bitch on the block could get their boosters to lift it for them when it debuted the next day.

He had to pay to play; she'd have to indulge his fantasies to get him to ante up.

As Carla allowed him to twist her limbs into pretzel positions and hump away, she reveled in the satisfaction of earning the man despite the odds. They'd grown up together, surviving a gang war that robbed them both of their siblings. Hustling was second nature where they were from; the boxing career Arron stumbled upon was supposed to be his ticket out but he never made enough to keep him out of the street life.

Juggling the two kept her man in the spotlight, for better or worse. Carla had no qualms about being his trophy piece, enjoying the spoils of his wars. They both played their position well; marrying his high school sweetheart on her was a shock but not a big deal in her long-term plans. His wife could keep the papers on him as long as she got all the extra cash and incentives of having the man.

Arron aggressively took her, grunting in carnal pleasures as he punished every available hole at his mercy. Silently, she took the punishment being at his complete disposal, knowing she had to do what the other women in his life would not. Fabricated lust coming from her lips resided in the comforting thought of enjoying his paycheck while his wife was left behind to cope with their trough of kids.

With each rough stroke she imagined the travels he afforded her. Arron flew her into every city he fought in, relishing their open secret within the confines of his coach and trainers on the road. Only girlfriends were allowed in the gym during training, and Carla whispered all the things in his ear he might have wanted to hear as his personal cheerleader. Their understanding became a thing that went beyond even their comprehension, and she went along eager for the ride.

Thinking about the pill breaking on her last month threw her concentration off.

Arron was thrilled like a kid in a candy store at the news of having a baby. Carla didn't want the crumb-snatcher cramping her style, but Arron could afford to make the experience lucrative. The thought of permanent paychecks covering child support and living expenses for the next twenty years helped her regain the swing in her hips he barely noticed had left.

Carla took a breath when Arron's body finally shook on top of hers and collapsed in defeat. Try as she might to get him up off of her, Arron took his time getting out of her honey-pot He wriggled in subjugated bliss against her while she adjusted to the creeping feeling in her gut she had before lust sidetracked her. She felt vulnerable in the chaos of his playfulness, and her attention focused to the nickel-plated pistol tucked between the seat.

Streets were talking. Rumor mills gossiped about Arron's vices. Everybody on the block knew cats were looking for him over unpaid debts. Gambling with high rollers in back alley establishments had caught up to him. The arrogance flaunting his purse money around in the faces of people that could barely hold water to snitch on his good fortune was care-less to her. The stone cold killers around the way were nothing to take lightly.

Playing the tough guy role, Arron laughed in the face of danger like the king of cool. Carla fed into his ego, telling him he was invincible even though she could see the hint of worry in his eyes he refused to admit to. Nor did she want him to; they would both have targets on their backs if he showed any weakness like that in the street. For both their sakes she fed into the lie to get her through the insecure seconds.

Much to Carla's relief, Arron got it together before the relaxation he felt from his release left him succumbing to a cat-nap. She hated being in the open with eyes watching in normal circumstances for this very reason, but Arron didn't believe in paying for motels. Backseats or the bathroom at a hole-in-the-wall they frequently partied in were their only two options for their encounters, and neither afforded her the privacy she liked.

Her worrying eased as he hurried to get dressed and back to their reality. They were behind schedule consummating their sin; his wife would be on the prowl for his whereabouts if he ran late far beyond a reasonable hour after the gym closed. Arron was in good spirits. He joked about baby names; Carla dropped hints on the colors for the purse. Like he always did after he got a piece he put some bread in her hand.

She counted it as he grinned; everything was everything.

Neither of them saw the old school roller with no lights on creeping up the block. Or the staccato fire bursts coming from its shadowed interior once it symmetrically aligned next to theirs. Carla heard sporadic shots shattering their windows before the pain registered she'd been hit. Joints between her shoulder blade ached something terrible within the seconds the roller screeched down the block and out of her focal point. But she was alive.

It never dawned on her, calling out to Arron, that he wouldn't be.

She spoke his name softly; he didn't respond, slumped over the steering wheel. Panic set in her spirit; ferociously, she shook him thinking he'd fainted. Sticky, wet liquids gushing from his wounds coated her hands like honey, dripping from her fingertips. A mass of splintered muscle, bone fragments, and clotting blood bubbled from the remnants of his face and neck. Carla checked his heartbeat; a shallow thump abruptly ceased.

Just like that, Carla knew Arron was gone.

For a brief moment she was paralyzed in shock at his passing; she'd seen dead bodies before in worse shape than his, just not as intimately. Deep breaths did little to calm her adrenaline but did control the hyperventilating. Nervously grabbing her phone, her first mind led her to call for help as if he could be saved. However, the consequences of being found in his company as a witness to murder in his wife's car kept her from connecting the call.

Instead, she called Merc, a trained field medic in Vietnam known for patching up the gunshot victims around the way who didn't have the luxury of hospital visits. He was quick and didn't ask any questions but was expensive and sewed up wounds without the benefit of anesthesia. Carla knew her pain tolerance was low, but a bottle of vodka and a blunt would be all she needed to cope with the pain when he stitched her up in the kitchen.

And it would cost Arron dearly as a parting gift for leaving her behind.

Carla picked through Arron's pockets like a common criminal, retrieving whatever remaining cash he had on him. The two grand she retrieved plus what he had already given her would be enough for her to make major moves later. Sirens began echoing from a couple blocks away, and Carla ditched her dead lover before she could be identified at the scene of the crime. Keeping off the sidewalks she detoured down uninviting alleys, forging through what lay ahead.

Calmly, she told herself she'd be cool; the unfortunate hard luck was just a temporary setback. All she needed to do was fight the feeling of passing out from blood loss and get home. Everything would be right as rain once she got the bullet out of her shoulder and figured out what her next move should be. Calls would have to be made to make sure she wasn't on anyone's list; once she was in the clear she could resume her hustle anew. The cash would last long enough to get a come up with heavy pockets. But first she had to make it to the sunrise.

And if she hurried in the morning, she could make it to Marshall Fields and get her purse with enough time and cash left over for an abortion.

◇◇◇◇◇◇

The Grass Beneath My Feet

S.A. Cosby

◇◇◇◇◇◇

Anyone who tell you that they don't mind going to jail is a goddamned liar. Oh, they'll tell you how much of an OG they are. They'll try and convince you how real they keep it. But what they won't tell you is how they lay on their back on top of their cot ever night silently crying in the dark as they stare up at the ceiling. Praying that tonight isn't the night a 300lb monster decides they have a pretty mouth. No, they won't tell you that. Jail is Hell on earth. And just like Hell it's filled with lost souls who have become demons. If you get a chance to find a way out of that Tartarus, you take it. Even if it's just to go see your mama laid out at the funeral home. You cherish those few hours like you're Persephone.

The Coldwater Correctional Facility van pulled up to the side door of a brick building that looked less like a mortuary and more like a bank. A short brother who hadn't missed a meal since 2003 opened the side door and spoke to Officer Hardy. I watched them through the corrugated steel grate that covered my window. The brother was nodding like his head was on a spring. Officer Hardy came back to the van and Officer Martinez turned towards me.

"All right, Turner, you know the drill. You straight with us we gonna be straight with you," he said. As prison guards go Martinez was all right. Hardy was a piece of shit who probably jerked off to torture porn. I nodded. Hardy opened the sliding door then

unlocked the inner cage door. Martinez stepped out
and helped me navigate my way out the van. I was
shackled at my ankles and my wrists. They hadn't
made me wear the waist chain because I hadn't had
any disciplinary issues in the last five years. That's
what passes as an accomplishment inside.

"Don't freak out when you see your dead mama,
Turner." Hardy said.

All heart that guy is.

We walked into a large chapel that was muted
browns and deep greens. Brown paneling on the
walls. Green valances that ran along the edge of the
ceiling. Dark green carpet. Sixty or seventy brown
wooden chairs. There was a small wooden pulpit to
the right. A huge picture of a redneck-looking white
Jesus was hanging on the wall behind the pulpit.

In front of the pulpit in a gray doeskin casket
was my mama.

The brother, who I assumed was the undertaker,
closed the door behind us. Hardy turned to him while
Martinez held me by the arm.

"Just so we're clear, there are no other family
members here, correct?" Hardy asked.

"No sir. We followed your instructions," the
undertaker said.

"Okay. You got an hour Turner," Hardy said.
Martinez let go of my arm. I took a deep breath. At
first, I couldn't move. My feet didn't want to work.
I looked down at the rug. It's so dark and green it
reminds me of grass. I haven't walked on grass in
fifteen years. Do you know how unnatural that is?
I ain't no granola-eating non-bathing vegan hippie
but even I know people are not meant to lose that
connection to the earth. I think that's why some
people inside go crazy. They're untethered from
the world. If you were like me you're never going to

feel the grass beneath your feet again. I'm doing an all-day bid. Big time. Life.

"Go ahead, Turner." Martinez whispered.

I took a few steps forward. My sister Wanda had made all the arrangements. I'm a little surprised she put her in such a cheap casket. Not for nothing, but doeskin is the human equivalent of burying a cat in a shoe box.

There is a sickly-sweet aroma coming from the coffin. Like strawberries that have gone bad. After a little while I recognize it. It's the cheap perfume my mama used to bathe herself in before heading out to a juke joint called Sharkey's with my father. When I was a kid it was the only place in our small southern town that catered to black folks. Every weekend they would leave me to watch Wanda while they went down to Sharkey's. They would come back stinking of liquor and bad decisions. Sometimes they came back kissing and sometimes they came back fighting like a pair of wild dogs.

I don't want to look at her. But I need to make sure she's dead.

I peer into the box. She's lost a lot of weight. The cancer has ravaged her body like a wildfire. It's devoured the curves she was so proud of. Her breasts are two hard cupcakes under a pink blouse. Her hands are crossed at her waist. Her face is slack like she's sleeping off a good drunk. I know what I'm supposed to feel. My mama is dead, and I'm supposed to be overcome with grief. But all I feel is a dull sense of relief. You want the long story? You won't get it from me. I'll give you the Cliff's Notes version. One night my mama stabbed my daddy and my dumb fifteen-year-old ass took the blame.

She said the police wouldn't believe it had been self-defense. They had a history of violence. A long history.

"But if you tell them you did it, Javon, they'll just think you was defending me. They won't send me to jail and we won't get split up. We all we got," she'd said to me as we sat on the floor near my daddy's still-warm body. A butcher knife stuck out of his chest like a flagpole. When I was fifteen her plan had made perfect sense. What could go wrong?

Everything, that's what. I got charged as an adult by an overzealous prosecutor who had his eye on the governor's mansion. It took the jury less than an hour to give me 25-to-life.

I ran my finger along her cheek. Her skin felt like candle wax.

The bible tells you to honor your mama and your father. But that big book of fairy tales doesn't tell you what to do when your mother gets you locked up on a murder bid. The first two years I was inside I stuck to the story. She assured me I'd get parole. I told myself I had to protect my mama. During my first appeal I kept my mouth shut. It was like I could see a floating neon sign above the judge's head that said, "PROTECT YOUR MAMA".

On the anniversary of my third year inside I got a letter from my sister. I hadn't heard from my mama in months. Wanda told me how CPS had put her in a foster home because our mama's new boyfriend couldn't keep his hands to himself. She also told me how my mom had collected on a life insurance policy for my daddy. She and her new boyfriend had moved into a brand new double-wide and were driving around town in a new truck.

I vomited in my cell after I finished reading her letter. I called my lawyer and told her everything. She filed a new appeal and this time I told the truth. And guess what? Nobody gave a fuck. Not the cops. Not the prosecutor who was now the governor. Least of all my mama, who was now married to her touchy-feely boyfriend.

As I stood next to the casket I felt the tears begin to fall. My whole body started to shake. I raised my head and looked at the picture of Gregg Allman Jesus. Where was he when a tiny fifteen-year-old boy was shoved into a cage full of beasts? I looked down at my mama again. She was wearing a pink blazer to go along with her pink blouse. Attached to the lapel of her blazer was a large papier-mache rose. I recognized that rose. It wasn't a brooch. It was a hat pin that my mother used as a lapel deco-ration. She never wore hats. She liked showing off her long black hair that she swore came from our indigenous ancestry.

I stared at that pin for a long time.

They are never going to let me go. My appeals ran out a long time ago. I'd given up my freedom for a woman who played me like a fiddle. A woman who had abandoned me in life. Maybe in death she could rescue me. Raise me from the depths of perdition on the petals of a rose.

I collapsed onto my mother's body. Hardy and Martinez didn't notice. They were busy debating the questionable outcome of last night's football game. My fingers danced over her chest. I slipped the pin under the handcuff on my left wrist. My orange jump-suit two sizes too big for me. The sleeves nearly came down to my fingertips. I straightened up and turned to face Hardy and Martinez.

"Hey yo, I'm ready," I said.

"You sure, Turner?" Martinez asked me. I heard he was a single dad of two little girls. Hardy is an ass at work, but I know he's big into the Knights of Columbus because he talks about it all the damn time. I push that shit out of my mind. I make myself go blank.

Hardy went to tell the undertaker we're leaving. Martinez took a position behind me. Hardy came back and opened the door. He had his back to me. I let the hat pin slip into my hand. Somewhere deep in my heart I hear the boy I used to be whisper "no."

But I'm doing this for him. For us.

I whirl around and stab Martinez in the eye. Eight inches of cheap steel slides through his eyeball and into his brain. It feels like I'm skewering a gum drop. I hear a soft gelatinous pop as I pull out the pin. Martinez stumbles backwards before crumpling to the floor. Hardy spins around. His eyes are as wide as dinner plates as he reaches for his gun. He's too slow. I leap forward and shove the pin into his throat just under his double chin. I shove him back against the door and it shuts with a bang. I pull out the pin and blood spews everywhere. Hardy puts both his hands on the wound but the blood seeps between his fingers. He slides down the door still clutching his throat. I grab the keys and unlock my restraints. I take Hardy's gun out of the holster just as the undertaker is peeping in the chapel.

"Give me your clothes and your car keys," I say. He nods enthusiastically.

He is one nodding motherfucker.

I lock him in a storage closet in the back of the mortuary. I put on his suit and leave through the front door. I never learned how to tie a necktie, so I leave it behind. I hop in the undertaker's Caddy. I silently thank my cousin Tay for teaching me to drive the summer before my daddy died.

After some fiddling I lower the window and turn on the radio. I don't recognize the song but that's all right. I hit the gas and leave the Coldwater Prison van in my rearview mirror. I know I won't get far. I know I probably won't make it out of this alive. But it doesn't matter right now. All I want to do is find a nice big field. I want to kick off these Sunday shoes and walk across that field barefoot. Feel the cool grass beneath my feet. Feel like I'm home.

◇◇◇◇◇◇

No News is Good News

Evelyn DeShane

◇◇◇◇◇◇

The dead body looked like a mannequin.

Marsha knew it was a silly thing to say. She'd watched a dozen true crime shows on Netflix and every single person who found a body always said that. They thought it was a mannequin in the river, or in the dump, or on the street. Never mind how horrifically out of context a mannequin in those places was, or the fact that mannequins were not proportioned like most people were; they insisted the sallow skin of a corpse was a mannequin before they made the grisly discovery. It always made Marsha think of her aunt's old consignment shop and how she'd spent her Saturdays as a teenager sorting through donation bins. Mannequins had been everywhere. She'd never mistaken any of those dead-eyed vacant stares for something human. No way.

But here she was, spouting the same cliché to the police officer as he interviewed her on her discovery.

"Are you okay, ma'am?" the officer asked. She noticed a twitch in his expression and a shift in his gait, as if he wanted to wrap his arms around her in a hug, but professional instinct told him not to. "Can I get you a glass of water?"

Marsha shook her head. She ran her long red nails through her black hair and tried to recreate the scene for him. Her clichés weren't going to cut it. So she started again from the beginning, from when she stepped out of the train station and turned the corner to the ravine by her bus stop. The officer, God, what was his name?—didn't bother to rewrite any of those details down. The bus stop was easy. So was crossing the street and noticing a red van pull away. She even remembered half the letters of the license plate: BRA. It was funny to her at the time and she had given those details to him quite easily.

But the body. It hung in her vision like a magic eye painting she could not bring into focus. "She was... un. I saw the red. Dress. And blood. And she looked so unreal."

"We know. That's a common response. We can interview about the rest later."

"No, no. I want to get this right." Marsha closed her eyes. There were no shoes on the body. That caught her attention first, because the toes seemed like they would be really cold. So I hadn't thought of her as a mannequin first, Marsha noted. It somehow made her feel better. She was aware of the humanity of the corpse; she wasn't an unfeeling monster.

She was able to get out her full description after that. The body had no shoes. The hair was blonde and matted, tangled into the bushes of the ravine. The woman's dress was open, displaying a chest that seemed to have no nipples. She didn't add that part to the description, though. She wanted to give the woman some dignity.

"You did really well. The license plate letters are going to help for sure," the officer said. He and Marsha both looked behind him as the body was lifted out of the ravine. Several workers became tangled in the bushes, struggling with the body. The dress ripped even more. From between her legs, Marsha noticed the penis. She thought it was another trick of the light at first, another way in which her vision had betrayed her and turned a human being into a mannequin.

But no, there was a penis. The woman was a trans woman.

The officer groaned, as if to echo her realization. "Another one?"

The other officers nodded their disdain. Marsha realized the way they handled the body now differed. They were careless, they were rough. The last strip of dignity was pulled back from the corpse. Marsha's eyes saw red.

"Another one?" she asked. "You have a serial killer?"

"No, ma'am. Nothing is wrong. Just a certain lifestyle leads to certain ends."

Marsha thought of the stab wound against the neck. Red like the woman's dress, artificial like her cause of death. Not a natural part of the lifestyle in the least. Though the officers had now covered up the corpse, the vision remained pressed to Marsha's third eye. She remembered the posters around the community centre from earlier in the week. The amount of women who seemed to go missing, and the women with stronger jawlines and names that didn't seem to match. Hazel. Andrea. And Violet.

A lifestyle injury. It seemed like a sick, cruel joke. As they loaded the body into the coroner van, a sickening sense of dread rolled through Marsha. "What do I do now?"

"Hmm?"

"What do you need me to do now? Will I be at a trial?"

The officer let out a low laugh that he quickly cut off as he realized the horror on Marsha's face. He put his notebook away in his back pocket. "Don't get ahead of the game. We still need to sort out what's gone on here. Find next of kin."

"And if you can't?"

"That's not your concern."

Marsha wanted to explain so much to him in that moment. But the sun was setting, it was getting dark, and her brother—her brother who used to be her sister, giving her access to understanding she never thought possible—was waiting for her to come home. "And after that?" Marsha pressed. "What is my concern?"

"Look," he said, his voice thin. "We will call if we need you. If you don't hear from us, consider it a good sign. You know the old saying? No news is good news. It applies here, too. You don't have to worry about this anymore."

The officer got into his car and slammed the door. Marsha tried to walk down the street, toward home, but glanced over her shoulder. The empty ravine haunted her.

Three days later, still without a phone call from the police to follow up, the ravine had grown over with a thin layer of snow. The white would cover everything. The silence would continue. Three more days passed with nothing. A week.

Marsha forgot about the mannequin woman until the next victim was found a month later. She was a nameless victim tossed inside an alleyway, only wearing a mini-skirt with a pink top. Tattoo of a dove on the left shoulder blade. The newspaper article laid out every last detail without actually saying anything at all. No transgender status was mentioned, but Marsha knew. Deep down, there could be no other way. She called the police station and found the officer who took her statement.

"I told you," he said, "we would call."

"I think you have a serial killer," she said. "There's another victim. She also doesn't have a name. But I think if you go through the missing people reports filed in the last little while, you'll find her. A lot of people from the Village have been going missing."

The officer didn't say anything. But she heard him breathing like a shadow behind her.

"You have to do something," she pressed. She's not the first and she won't be the last.

"We are doing all we can."

"That's..." Marsha closed her eyes. That was precisely what she was afraid of. The police were doing all they could, and it still amounted to nothing. She saw the woman—the mannequin—again. Her eyelids. "What was her name?"

"Hmm?"

"The woman I found. What was her name? Did anyone bury her? I want to see."

"Ronald Black," he said after a while.

"That's not her name."

"We don't have any other information at this time."

"But what was her name?"

When the officer only gave her silence, Marsha eventually hung up.

◇◇◇◇◇◇

"Jessica?"

"Look again, sir," Jesse said. He splayed his legs to make his hips seem less wide, and his shoulder more broad. He cursed himself for shaving. The dusting of hair on his upper lip was never that much, but it at least signalled more than his still-out-of-date license ever could. "It's not Jessica."

The convenience store owner glanced down again. He shrugged. "Jesse. Sure. What year were you born?"

"1988." Jesse beamed. "I'm twenty-nine."

"You look barely nineteen."

"But I'm twenty-nine. Born July 7th 1988. I can give you my mother's date of birth too. Maybe her maiden name and the street I grew up on as a child. Will that convince you it's not a fake ID?"

The store owner's stare turned from hardened to defeated. He tossed the ID back on the counter and turned to open a case where the cigarettes were kept. If not for the shaking hands Jesse got right before therapy, he would have avoided this place. He never passed in these kinds of stores. He was convinced it was the fluorescent lights, the cameras and mirrors around every corner. People were so prone to see theft in stores like this, or conning through fake IDs, that each and every last feminine mannerism still not yet worked out of him was highlighted and suspect.

But he knew it was really his ID. He glanced at the photo of himself two years ago, barely on testos-terone, and the F marker where sex was listed. What on earth was the point of changing his damn name if people still saw a girl's one instead? What was the point of having any official ID with a brand new name if there still was a giant F in the centre of the thing? It was always the F that made people's sanity fall away. Always the damn F. Apple cheeks and small hands could be reasoned away by shitty genetics. But an F left no room to doubt his origins. Jesse Martinez was trans.

Jesse lit up his cigarette outside of the store. He should have been smoking at least nine metres away, but he wanted to show some disrespect back for what he'd just received. When Talia, a tall trans woman with a mini-skirt on walked by him, she splayed her hand in a wave.

"You comin' tonight, hon?"

"You know it. Not exactly like we have a choice."

"We always have a choice. It's just not the easy one, you dig?" When he said nothing in response, she gestured to his cigarette. "You mind tossing me one, honey?"

"As long as you stop calling me honey, then we have a deal."

"Pfft." She waved her hand away like it was nothing. Her dismissal grated on his nerves, but he figured he could spare a cigarette. She was one of the most talkative in group; he knew all her secrets if he really wanted to harm her. Talk a bit more about her grandmother whose name she wanted to honour, but who had spit in her face when she came out as trans. Talia was also one of the favourites of Genie, the therapist who would eventually sign thee letters approving their surgery. Jesse figured he would get brownie points just from being nice to her; gate-keeper acceptance via osmosis.

"So how are you and your boy?" Talia asked, trying to make small talk. "I hear he dropped out."

"He did. Yes." Jesse didn't want to talk about Anthony's betrayal, as he thought of it. He knew it wasn't a reflection of him or their relationship, but it was hard to accept no longer seeing Anthony in therapy. Anthony now had family money that would allow him to obtain surgery privately. A sister who would help him out when it came time to heal and help him out again if he ever lost his job because of his trans status. He had no use for the therapy sessions that mostly turned into a despair circle jerk. Jesse and Anthony had met bonding over their hatred of events like this, while also lamenting the therapist's necessary role in their lives if they wanted to live their lives as they wished as men. Jesse thought they'd shared a fantasy together about a world that would bend to their whim as soon as they got surgery; the city would be theirs, and they could take it over from all the cissies who had made them feel like shit.

Instead, Anthony was about to join the rank of the cissies. And Jesse, like always, was left to nurse his fantasies alone.

He took a long drag on the cigarette. Talia was reminiscing about group therapy as if it was fucking summer camp, talking about how much she loved Anthony's jokes and dry humour. She didn't seem to think it a hardship that he wasn't there anymore, or that therapy itself wasn't the most invasive and cloying experiences.

"You don't find it strange?" Jesse asked after a moment. "Spilling all our secrets to this place?"

"Nah. Just tell them what they want to hear and you get what you want."

"But it's not that simple."

"It can be if you let it. Remember Genie's advice from the first day? No news is good news. We should strive to be boring. We should strive for normal." Talia laughed while Jesse huffed. "It may be antiquated nonsense, but it's also kind of true. We need to just get our letters and move on. We don't need to make headlines, you know? Life doesn't have to be as hard as you make it out to be.

Jesse stared at the dirt in front of them, his mind reeling. How could any of this be easy? He'd just been called Jessica. He'd always be called Jessica because it looked just close enough to Jesse. He could change his name and start all over again, but even the most masculine name didn't matter if his body was found. They'd peel back the cloth-ing and find a vagina. They'd examine the bones and see child-bearing hips. He was fucked in this life and

---

fucked because there was nothing beyond this one. He would always make the headlines, but it would never be in the gender he wanted.

"You're always pouting," Talia complained. She stamped out her cigarette and gestured for them to walk. "I mean, you don't even have it that bad."

"I don't?"

"Yeah," Talia said, cutting him off before he could rant. "Have you even noticed just how many trans women go missing? We're being pegged off, one by one, because we're the gender fodder. The gender monsters. So people kill us. Trans men don't get that."

"Brandon—"

"Don't even say Brandon Teena because that was a lesbian story. He wasn't killed for being a man but fucking someone's woman. That's it."

Jesse wanted to scream. White-hot rage built inside of him and only cooled as he light another cigarette. Talia kept citing sources about trans women as monstrous, quoting the never-wrong Susan Stryker and Julia Serano. All names he knew. All theories he was familiar with. And really, all points that were valid. Trans women did disappear.

But so did trans men. They just disappeared in different ways than trans women, and no one fucking bothered to see it. Either they disappeared into their former feminine identities through lack of institutional recognition or they passed well enough to disappear into masculinity. Until their pants came off, of course. Jesse thought of all the ways in which he'd studied cis men in high school from afar, attempting to affect masculinity like a role he could slip into. The silent head nods, the flexing in mirrors, the quiet complacency. Trans men disappeared into hormones, into the rage that came more easily and the muscles that clenched underneath skin, but it all fell apart once pants were removed and once that skin was peeled back.

Trans women were murdered, sure, he could accept that. But trans men became silent monsters.

Jesse stamped out the last bit of his cigarette before he entered the building. In the basement of a community centre, a group of sixteen trans people in the midst of their transitions all faced one another in a circle. They gave their names and preferred pronouns before the leader in the centre—always cis, always a medical professional—directed them. They were all pawns in a game. All playing a role.

When Genie called on Talia, she stood up and spoke eloquently. She smiled. She gestured. She was successful in the role and she knew it. It would take another couple weeks, but Jesse knew Talia would get approved for surgery. She would live the rest of her life as a woman. No one would disagree. She would make no headlines. No news would be good news, like Genie always said. Strive for boring. Strive for normal.

When it was his turn, he mumbled. He grunted. He did not emote enough. He failed Genie's test of confessional therapy, but he knew he passed his own. His masculinity covered him like another skin, like a mask that hid his fantasies.

"Well, that was fun," Talia said once the meeting was over. "I suppose I'll see you next week."

"Yeah, something like that."

Jesse smoked as he watched Talia wander down the street. He fingered the knife in his pocket he always carried for self-defense. After he put out his cigarette, he followed behind Talia silently.

"I think something's wrong," Anthony said. He stared into the mug of coffee in front of him. The whipped cream topping had seemed too girly when he ordered it, something that Jesse would have lectured him about if he had been here. He should have been here, but he cancelled at the last minute in a sparse text. Anthony never thought he'd miss the gender-passing nitpicking so much.

Marsha leaned forward on her chair. She extended her hand to Anthony, squeezing him gently. "Want to talk about it?"

"Well, yeah. It's just hard. I know you don't believe me when I say that testosterone has wiped my memory of feeling words, but it's kind of true."

Marsha chuckled lightly. "Oh, I believe it. I just don't think it's purely chemical. It's cultural."

"Sure. Maybe it's both. The truth is often in the middle."

"So what's the middle of what you're worried about? Chances are, it's not benign, but it's probably not as big of a thing as you're making it out to be."

Anthony bit his lip. "I think he's cheating."

"Oh, no sweetie. No." Marsha's face softened. She squeezed his hand again as he went through all the evidence he'd accumulated. Jesse was moodier now than ever before. Already cranky to begin with, it was as if he was riding a wave of ups and downs that would not relent. He'd be sullen and not speak or leave his room for days. Then he'd disappear and come back with manic energy. He wasn't kissing Anthony nearly as much anymore, either. When he did, it was much rougher, and often coupled with his manic periods.

"And he's been going out for longer and longer, sometimes without calling or warning, Anthony said. "He's missing dates like this, too.

"And you're sure it can't be anything else? Maybe he's got a new job or a side gig to help pay for things? I know his parents haven't been great. Maybe he's trying to reconcile with them?"

"Not a chance," Anthony said, laughing a little. ""I think he'd kill his parents if he knew he could get way with it."

Marsha blinked. Anthony instantly regretted the words. "Sorry. Not to be so grim. It's just—"

"No, it's fine. I need to strengthen my stomach anyway." Marsha took a shaky drink from her coffee cup. Silence enveloped them. It felt like a wound.

Anthony had heard about the woman in the ditch on the night it happened. He'd dreamed about a graveyard full of mannequin arms between tombstones. When the next woman was found, he'd had the dream again. At first he didn't want to mention the next missing woman poster he'd seen around the city, thinking it would trigger Marsha, but she called him and told him about it. She'd found several more cases too, all trans women, all of whom had gone missing without a trace or been found without being ID'd.

"Any more news?" Anthony asked tentatively.

"Some, yeah. I mean the police aren't helping but I think that the numbers are not as big as I once thought."

"Oh?"

"No. Because the police work with legal names or don't find the names to begin with, it's been hard to match up the victims with the missing. But there is overlap and I'm convinced I'm finding it. The numbers are going down. Not much, but some.

"That's... good." Anthony tried to drink his coffee. The words he wanted to say hung between them like a secret dream language that they'd once shared as sisters but had spread out and dispersed since his transition. She was always going to be there for him, but she was always going to be haunted by the negatives of this life. The murder and violence. Jesse's parents abandoning him and the doctors mistreating him. As much as he wanted her to see the better parts of this community, he was coming up on blanks.

"I still haven't found her name, though," Marsha added. "Which still makes me sad."

"I know. I'm sorry. You've done far more than anyone could have."

"But that's the thing. It shouldn't be me but the cops." She sighed and ran her hands through her dark hair. Her nail polish was chipped, the nailbed itself marked with flaked dry skin and red scabs from picking too much. Marsha forced a smile. "So let's not talk about that. Let's talk about your issue. Have you tried talking to Jesse?"

Anthony shook his head. "I could. I mean... Nothing is stopping me."

"But?"

"But I think right now I'm becoming that cop that told you no news was good news. You know a therapist once said it to us, too?"

"Oh, really? That's..."

"Gross, I know. But it also makes a strange type of sense. No news is good news. Don't rock the boat. Strive for boring, strive for normal." Anthony sighed. He glanced down at his chest, still inside a compression binder, and wondered what it would feel like flat. His surgery appointment was in six weeks. Would Jesse still want to fuck him then? Or would his jealousy take over?

Suddenly, the fog lifted from his vision. Marsha noted and raised her eyebrows in suggestion. "You okay?"

"Yeah, I think I figured it out, though. All of this started to happen when Jesse heard about the surgery money I had. When I dropped out of therapy. He's...jealous. He wants what I have so much more, but doesn't have a family who will help."

"He has you, though. He should be happy about that."

"He does, but I need to show him. More than before. Oh." Anthony sighed, feeling relief wash over him. "This is perfect. Thank you so much for talking, Marsh."

"I didn't do much." She shrugged and then held her arms out for a hug. Anthony embraced her easily and squeezed her tight. Under her large winter sweater, he could feel that she was all sharp angles and bones. She was losing weight. But he said nothing about it.

"Call me tonight?" she asked. "Let me know you're okay?"

"How about I call you if something goes wrong?" he suggested, then winked. "You know, no news is good news."

Though Marsha rolled her eyes, she also let him go with another squeeze.

Though a part of him wanted to tell her to eat something more than coffee, he wouldn't. She was his older sister. She knew what she was doing.

When Anthony came into the apartment that he shared with Jesse, he found him already there. Jesse stood at the sink, his back stiff. He wore the same pair of jeans as earlier in the day, but he had on no shoes or socks. Dirt was caked onto the front hall mat. Anthony suppressed what he was going to say in greeting when he noticed pats of blood mixed in with the dirt. He moved into the kitchen and noticed blood marking the back of Jesse's shirt.

"Oh my God. Are you okay?"

A dozen scenarios repeated in his mind. Hilary Swank from Boys Don't Cry,

Drew Barrymore from the opening sequence of Scream. When he examined Jesse's face under the low kitchen light, he saw no injuries. Jesse's eyes seemed vacant, his expression immovable.

"You're home early."

"I am," Anthony said. "But I thought you wouldn't be home at all."

"Well, I am."

Jesse's voice was like ice. It made the hair at the back of Anthony's neck stand up. When he looked at Jesse's hands, he saw blood mixed with soap, runny with water. A knife lined the kitchen sink. The blood on his shirt had no origin, no trace of a wound.

Still, Anthony asked if he was okay again.

"I'm fine. Just a little scratch. Nothing to worry about."

"Okay." Anthony didn't remove his eyes from the bloodstain. "Are you sure? If something happened, you know you can tell me, right?"

"I know. I would."

"Good."

Silence stretched between them. The din of the running water hitting the metal basin became too much. When Jesse turned it off, all the blood from the knife was gone. So was the soap and pink suds on his hands. The only speck of gore that remained was the blood-stained shirt. Jesse seemed like he wanted to remove it, but couldn't.

Because he doesn't have a binder on, Anthony realized. His breasts were visible. Tightly bound with a sports bra instead of a compression tank, but still visible. And he is ashamed.

"I need some privacy," Jesse said.

"Right. Of course."

Jesse nodded. He left the kitchen for their shared bedroom around the corner. Anthony stood in the kitchen. He put his hands on the sink and looked at the knife. It was not a kitchen knife, like he once thought, but one that he'd seen in Jesse's bag in the past. The one for self -defense. He repeated Jesse's claims of self-defense over and over. Anthony suppressed all other dawning thoughts. He heard Jesse shift and change in the other room.

"I have something I want to tell you," Anthony said.

Jesse didn't say anything.

Anthony went on. "I was talking to Marsha and I realized that I was being unfair. I should have shared my surgery money with you."

The shifting stopped. Jesse's breath was heavy. "What do you mean?"

"I should have split it with you. That way we both work together to get what we need."

Jesse appeared in the doorway. The blood was no longer visible. Every trace of what Anthony had just witnessed was now gone, and because it was easier, he let it disappear. In between the two extremes, the answer was somewhere in the middle. Jesse was moody because he missed out on surgery. That was that. Everything else wasn't important.

"Are you serious?" Jesse asked.

"Yes. We're in this together, okay?"

Jesse wrapped him in a hug. It was rough, like usual, but there was tenderness inside it as well. Anthony was sure. The two of them were happy. Their lives were taking shape together; he should have been focused on them as a unit, on their shared fantasy, rather than anything else.

"Are you going to be okay?" Anthony asked, after the hug was over.

Jesse didn't answer; he merely put the knife that had once been in the sink back into his pocket, and then took Anthony to the couch.

Anthony decided to take the silence as good news.

◇◇◇◇◇◇

The Bag Girl

Alec Cizak

◇◇◇◇◇

Her supervisor, working the express lane, summoned her. "Bag girl," he said. He snapped his fingers. She wondered if he even knew her name, if he'd ever bothered to read the plastic tag pinned to her black apron.

But she hustled over. Tough to get a job in Haggard these days. Especially for a high school drop out with nothing to offer but a smile and quick hands. She grabbed a paper sack from a stack at the end of the second conveyor belt and loaded the customer's groceries. The customer slid his card into the credit machine and typed his secret code. Her supervisor asked him, "You want big bills, or little bills?"

"Twenties'll be fine," said the customer.

Her supervisor counted out five and handed them over, along with the receipt. The customer grabbed his eggs and bananas. He didn't hide his effort to peek into the bag girl's button-down dress shirt underneath her apron. She grinned, played along. She eased her hand into her back pocket and worked the keypad on an ancient BlackBerry phone—*Bears jersey, khakis, boat shoes, dbag*.

The next customer's wardrobe must have come off the bargain rack at Walmart, a t-shirt with a bald eagle on it flying over the words,*Don't Tell Me How To Freedom!*, and grease-stained jeans tucked into cowboy boots. On his hip, he wore a holster and handgun, just like those tea party dorks on television. When he spoke, he barely moved his thin lips, like being civil to another human being demanded too much. She asked him if he wanted his six-pack in a bag.

"Do your job," he said to her.

She stuffed the beer into a paper sack and handed it to him as he walked by her. He didn't look at her, didn't ogle her cleavage. No matter. For the moment, the man meant nothing. He'd paid for his Budweiser with coins he'd dropped from a coffee can cradled under his arm.

Time crawled while she whipped groceries into bags and said, "Have a nice day," like a robot. The automatic doors to her right opened and the guy in the Bears jersey stumbled into the store, holding his blood-stained hands to the side of his head. He spilled into two rows of shopping carts, fell on his knees and wept.

Her supervisor scratched at a Cuba-shaped meth scab on his forearm. He said, "Dammit, not again!"

◇◇◇◇◇◇

Her boyfriend used the money to score a baggie of vikes. They each popped two and plopped down in front of his old fashioned, humpbacked television. The news talked about the hits at the super market. Three nights over the last two weeks. She'd only been with her boyfriend for a month when he'd come up with the plan. He'd found prepaid BlackBerry phones at a Quick 'N' Go outside of Pawpaw Grove. "This routine won't last long," he'd said. "Soon as the pigs catch on, we crack the phones and ditch them in Lake Arthur."

The first time they'd tried the scam, she'd doubted they'd pull it off. If her boyfriend got caught, she'd slip the phone into a customer's bag when they weren't looking. But things went smooth. Several customers shrieked from the parking lot. The cops showed. Then an ambulance and a fire truck. All for a normal guy who'd taken two shots to the face from a solid steel meat tenderizer. Yes, it cracked his skull a little but, you know, so what? He had money. She and her boyfriend didn't. Her boyfriend had been stealthy, moved in from behind the security cameras, dressed in black, wearing a ski mask. He smacked the guy twice with the metal mallet, reached into his back pocket, and ripped out his wallet. He'd been gone before anyone noticed the normal guy slumped over, bleeding onto the trunk of a cream-colored BMW.

That night, they'd celebrated, big time. Their man sold them some Oxy and they crushed and snorted it. Everything went fine until they tried to have sex. Her boyfriend's penis lay still, like a bored slug. She said, "That's all right, I understand." For whatever reason, this infuriated him. He punched the wall and shouted at his crotch.

He said, "You piece of shit!" She suspected he'd meant to cuss at her. The wall, even, might have been a stand-in.

They stretched the first guy's money for almost a week. Then they had to pull another hit. Similar target—Clean haircut, wedding ring, golf shirt, square face, smug expression of superiority when he glanced down the bag girl's shirt as he took his groceries. She didn't feel bad when he'd collapsed on the sidewalk, just outside the store.

The haul from the second guy didn't match the first. They tried to make the pills last as long as possible. As the baggie emptied, her boyfriend's temper blossomed. She did her best to get him going in bed. He must have been on dope a lot longer than her. His thing refused to respond. She only wanted to help. He finally shoved her to the floor and called her a bitch. "You see the fucker won't stand, don't you?" Like it was her fault.

The news report suggested the Lake County sheriff's department would establish a task force to catch the Supermarket Bandit, a name decided upon by the normal people of Haggard. She said to her boyfriend, "This is getting serious." She suggested they take it easy for a while.

"That makes no sense," said her boyfriend. He grabbed her hair and jerked her head toward him. "I need you to think," he said. "Don't get goofy on me."

She said, "I don't want to do it anymore."

At this, her boyfriend's pockmarked face stilled. He said, "You walk away, I'll rat out the both of us."

She understood, then, her inability to plan ahead formed the foundation of all her problems in life. In high school, she'd partied and screwed around, as opposed to staying at home and studying, like normal people, the ones who now lived in houses, had children, new cars, mortgages, all the things normal people were supposed to have; When she'd started using pills every day, her conscience told her it might not be a good idea. She'd tried to quit, once. No way she'd go through that hell again—walls closing in, like the trash compactor scene in that stupid Star Wars movie normal people gushed on about. One of the boys she'd snagged in high school had, despite his good looks, been on the chess team. He explained to her how chess and life were the same. He said, "Every move you make, you must consider every possible counter. If you don't, you're dead."

◇◇◇◇◇◇

The bag girl and her boyfriend gobbled the vikes over the next four days. Then her boyfriend told her, "We're going to need to borrow some more money tonight."

She attempted, once more, to convince him it might not be a good idea. "They got cop cars prowling by every five minutes," she said. "At least twice an hour, the pigs park in front of the store, get out, and stroll through the parking lot. It's totally uncool." Of course, she'd said the same thing every night since the task force had been created.

"I think we can get away with it," he said. "You just send me customers. If shit looks cool, I'll take care of business. If not, I'll hang back and wait for your next message."

"I really don't think it's smart," she said.

Her boyfriend's chest, covered in half-finished tattoos, heaved to an exaggerated rhythm. He looked like a man about to speak his final words. He said, "Is this going to get ugly?" His hands transformed into fists, his giant, walnut-sized knuckles doing what his penis couldn't—stranding firm. Something in his neck creaked and popped as he turned to face her. The bridge of his nose wrinkled.

She said his name. She said, "Please don't make me. . ."

Before she finished, he grabbed her hair and twisted her sideways. His free hand, still closed in a tight, shaking fist, hovered over her. "Bitch," he said, his thin lips pursed like the redneck in the store with the gun on his belt, "I'm tired of you thinking you got some kind of choice."

She wished she could have summoned the strength of the gods right then and blasted her boyfriend in the mouth. The more she resisted, the tighter he gripped her. His other arm trembled, as

TOUGH

though building steam. She didn't want him to know
he'd scared her. She said, in halting, choking words,
"Okay, okay. . ."

When her boyfriend let her go, she said she
needed to get ready for work. She'd been with jerks
before, but none of them had anything on her, not
like this one. How long would she go away for? Would
she be able to score dope in prison? What sort of
awful shit would the bad girls in jail make her do for
a fix? She ducked into the shower and wept as she
ran a paper-thin piece of soap over her body. She
lathered up the rest of the soap and used it to wash
her hair. She tried dressing in the bathroom, alone.
Her boyfriend insisted on keeping the door open.
He leaned against the wall and stared at her. She
wiped steam from the mirror above the sink with
the cardboard tube from a dead roll of toilet paper.
She spoke to her boyfriend through the mirror. She
said, "What?"

He didn't say anything, just bored into her with
his half-open, bloodshot eyes.

◇◇◇◇◇◇

Friday night. Normal people came into the store
angling for fresh money from their bank accounts.
Almost every other customer opted for cash when
they ran their debit cards. Eighty bucks here, a
hundred there, over and over. She offered her
boyfriend one sacrificial yuppie after another. None
returned with a bloodied face and empty pockets.
Every time she glanced outside the giant window at
the front of the store, a squad car either rolled by
in the street or crept through the lot. On her break,
she squatted near empty fruit crates behind the
store and smoked a cigarette. One of her coworkers,
a crumbling meth junkie who resembled a straggler

from Dawn of the Dead, talked on his cell phone. He finished his conversation and went back inside. From the shadows between spotlights mounted on the roof of the store, her boyfriend snaked up and hissed at her. "How about sending me something when the place isn't crawling with pigs?"

She shrugged. "What am I supposed to do?"

He wrapped his crooked fingers around the top of her button-down shirt. She dropped her generic cigarette as he hoisted her to a standing position. "You think you can survive an empty night?" He didn't let her speak. "We both know the answer." Maybe she sneered at him. Whatever look came across her face, it compelled him to tap her cheek with his monster knuckles. He said, "I'll make this simple for you. You pay close attention to the lot and give me a goddamn customer when things are obviously cool. You take care of this real soon, or I'm going to call the cops and tell them I saw the bag girl texting someone before the last hit."

This stunned her worse than the back of his hand. She said, "I'm on it. I promise."

◇◇◇◇◇◇

Closing time approached and she still hadn't found a good prospect in conjunction with a cop-free parking lot. Plenty of normal people asked for money, like they hadn't seen the news, like they didn't know what could be waiting for them outside. She wondered if her boyfriend would be bold enough to march into the store and confront her. She imagined him pacing the alley separating the store and the nightclub behind it. Maybe he'd punched the night-club's brick wall a few times. Or maybe he'd used the meat tenderizer to chip away at it, thinking about the horror of sweating through the night without

147

a fix. Around eleven-thirty, a normal guy in one of those musclehead shirts, the kind with ornate writing nobody could read, swiped his card and collected a stack of ten-dollar bills. Hardly any cars in the parking lot. No cops anywhere. The bag girl reached into her pocket, ready to text. Then she heard coins, rattling in a coffee can. The man with the gun on his belt counted out change for a six-pack three aisles down. He'd worn his gun again. His Walmart t-shirt, this time, said, *I Loves Me Some 2nd Amendment!* The bag girl made sure she described the man's cowboy boots and his dirty jeans as she texted her boyfriend.

The next customer in her line, a normal woman in a tank-top and shorts showing off her perfect, unblemished thighs, told her to keep her yogurt and celery separate. The bag girl said, "Sure thing, ma'am." Five pops, like firecrackers, erupted outside. She didn't even turn her head as everyone else in the store, including the normal woman, craned their necks to see what had happened. The bag girl dropped the BlackBerry phone into the normal woman's paper sack, right next to her yogurt. As the normal woman passed, refusing to make eye contact with her, the bag girl said, "Have a wonderful evening."

◇◇◇◇◇◇

Sarah, Sweet and Stealthy

Preston Lang

◇◇◇◇◇◇

Two years earlier, the Poet Laureate of Delaware stole a 95,000-dollar table from Jean's parents' dining room. She'd met him at a bar when she was still a year too young to drink legally. Her friend Robbie introduced him as Samson, an old pal from lacrosse camp. She danced with this Samson, a dark-eyed beauty with terrific forearms. He drove a red pickup truck and knew how to nae-nae. While he was off getting her a drink, Robbie mentioned that he was actually the Poet Laureate of Delaware, but he didn't like to tell people because it seemed like bragging and he'd feel pressure to be lyrical all the time. But Samson barely talked. He just wanted to get out on the dance floor and press her close. And when he needed her to follow him, he'd gesture sensually with his forefinger.

Jean's parents were out of town for the long weekend, so she took that laureate home to her mom's queen-sized where they went at it, on and off, for about three hours. When she woke up the next morning, he was gone, but he'd left a note: *Sarah, sweet and stealthy, I will always remember you.* Did he really think her name was Sarah? Or was that some literary reference? She just didn't know.

It was only after breakfast that she realized one of the dining room tables, the one they didn't eat on, was gone. It was a limited-edition Rheinspahn, and it had cost her stepfather nearly a hundred grand. When her parents got home, she pled ignorance. "Someone must have stolen it in the night—*isn't that scary*." It didn't seem like such a big deal to Jean. The thing was insured. And anyone who could afford to drop 95 grand on a table he didn't eat on could afford to lose it. Her stepdad accused her of being in on the crime, though he didn't bring that suspicion to the police. Her mother called Jean a spoiled, irresponsible dropout, living in unearned luxury. The fight, a long time in coming, was big and vicious. Ugly things were said that couldn't really be taken back because they were so obviously true. A lot of hair was pulled. Jean took a knee to the stomach.

She'd been on the road ever since, staying on couches when she was lucky, meeting some interesting people and some very dull people, making lots of spectacular mistakes. She lost an incisor, and in the winter she was always sick.

One January night she found herself standing outside a bookstore in Wilmington where she saw a sign in the window for a poetry reading: three local writers, including the Poet Laureate of Delaware. First the non-titled authors read. Jean didn't understand any of it. Even words she thought she knew well—*gift, remains, shortchange*—were used in ways she just didn't get. It all felt mean-spirited and wrong, but no one did anything to stop it.

The laureate went last. She was a wide, silver-haired lady named Elaine Lind. She read a poem about being stuck in an elevator with a spider and then one about learning to French-kiss at Dunkin' Donuts. Jean didn't really know whether she liked the poems, but there was something agreeable and perceptive in the woman's eyes, she thought.

When it was over, the two other poets had friends and relatives. The laureate had no one, but it didn't seem to bother her. She loaded her plate with cheese and slices of ham then sat in a folding chair near the back.

"In the elevator poem I'm glad that the spider didn't start to talk," Jean said to her.

Elaine Lind nodded. "Yes, a talking animal is almost always a bad idea. In a poem."

Soon after, they were drinking wine together under a poster of John Grisham, and Jean told the whole story—the laureate, the night in mom's bed, the stolen table.

"How heavy was the table?" Elaine asked.

"How heavy?"

"Yes. An estimate."

"It wasn't huge, but it was solid. I don't know."

"Could one man carry it out by himself?"

"Maybe a really strong guy."

"You said he had nice forearms. What's the word they use? Shredded? Was he all shredded, ripped, frayed, ruptured?"

"He was a strong guy. Maybe he could've done it alone."

"I'm just wondering if he would have needed a partner."

They were able to look up the table online. It weighed 170 pounds.

"I weigh 170 pounds," Elaine said. "A strong man could easily carry me out of a dining room. The truck he drove: Delaware plates?"

"No. I remember they were Connecticut plates. Local, you know."

"Maybe they spelled something clever, like Laureate69?"

"No. Sorry. Nothing I could remember."

"That's all right. Did you tell him about the table? You know, the night before, how much it was worth?"

"I don't remember. But I might have. I thought it was so stupid: a 95,000-dollar table. And I liked to tell people about the really stupid things my parents did."

On the laureate website, there was no one named Samson, and a look through the past 15 years of pictures didn't turn up anything either.

"Why are there so many of them?" Jean asked.

"The term is only six months. Not only that, for the past eleven years there have been two laureates at a time."

"Why?"

"Some feud between the governor's office and the state arts council. It's not important. Did you ever ask your friend Robbie about that night?"

"What do you mean?"

"The friend who introduced you."

Jean had never thought to do that, an obvious first step. Then again she hadn't really cared about the table or finding Samson. Now she did. It wasn't hard to track down Robbie's phone number. He worked a PR job in New York, and he answered on the first ring, happy to talk to a pretty girl from the old days.

"Yeah, I'd never met the guy before. He saw me talking to you, and he said he'd buy me a drink if I'd introduce him to you as an old friend. Then he said he'd buy me two more if I told you that he was chief poet of Louisiana or something."

"Delaware."

"Okay, Delaware. Did you go home with him?"

The poet laureate wrote on a slip of paper—
Details about Samson.

"Can you tell me anything else about this guy? His real name, where he was from?"

"I don't really remember much about him. Handsome guy, though. Wouldn't think he'd have to play games to pick up girls. Hey, what's this about?"

Jean got off the phone, and for some reason she was a little embarrassed.

"I don't want you to think that I—you know—that I do that kind of thing all the time."

"What? Hook up with boys?"

"Yeah."

"Nothing to be ashamed of. A few weeks ago, I had sex with a man who sells shrooms out of his car."

"Did you do it *in* the car?"

"Yes, actually. We made love in his Saab. *We made love in his sob?* No, that doesn't work." Elaine shook off the bad verse. "No, what matters is finding the man who stole your table. Let me think."

The bookstore was closing up, so they went to a bar down the block where they drank cheap vodka.

"I just don't think someone claims to be Poet Laureate of Delaware out of nowhere. There's something behind that," Elaine said. "*Sarah, Sweet and Stealthy*? Are you sure that's what he wrote?"

"Yes, I kept it for a while. The scrap of paper. I lost it somewhere."

Jean didn't retain possessions. At the moment, all she had was a small purse that she'd found—no cash, no wallet—outside a Burger King just before sunup about a week earlier.

"It must be from somewhere," Elaine said.

They did a simple search for the phrase, but nothing came up.

"I've got a friend out at UD. He might know something, and even if he doesn't, we can use his password to get into the journal database."

"What's that?"

"It's got a ton of small literary journals on it, and we can do a phrase check on Sarah, sweet and stealthy."

"It checks every little magazine?"

"Not every single one, but a lot of them."

Elaine texted Dr. Sohn. He wrote back right away. He was still awake—come on over.

"Is it close?" Jean asked.

"It's Delaware, dear. Everything is close."

Dr. Sohn was about 70, a short man in an ancient bathrobe.

"But we have to keep it down. Dahlia is asleep," he said.

They gave him as much of the story as he needed to know. Dr. Sohn looked very familiar to Jean. It was as if she'd seen his face in connection with something dishonest and ugly.

"Why are you looking at me like that?" Dr. Sohn said.

"I've seen you before. I think."

Jean felt tense, a little angry. On the road, she'd started to develop a sense, a very imperfect sense, of when she needed to bolt.

"Oh, I know," Elaine said with a little laugh. "You were looking at his picture only an hour ago."

He'd been laureate twelve years earlier.

"Yeah, I did my six months," he said. If you're a published poet in the state of Delaware you've probably been laureate at some point."

"The best part is when you accidentally rhyme and someone says *you're a poet and don't even know it*, you can just kind of give them a look," Elaine added.

Dr. Sohn poured out coffee.

"Sarah, sweet and stealthy," he said carefully.

They searched the phrase on the database. Nothing came up.

"Any students stand out to you: good-looking, fit?" Elaine asked.

"Always a lot of handsome boys. But none of them were fit until the late 80s. 1987, a guy comes into my class with deltoids." He stirred cream into his cup. "I have to say, though, the *sweet and stealthy* line. It does sound familiar."

"Like something a student wrote for class?"

"No, I feel like it's something I read, not something I heard out loud, which rules out anything a student wrote."

"You don't read your student's work?"

"Not for the past eight years. If they don't read it in class, I don't know about it."

"So we should check the journals not in the database?"

"And I would start eight years ago and work back."

"You stopped reading journals too?"

"The only poetry I read now is John Donne."

"So you haven't read anything of *mine* in the past eight years?"

"Elaine, I love you, but I'm not going to read your words."

Just then a very tired woman came into the kitchen in a thick nightgown.

"What is all this?"

"Sorry, we'll try to be more quiet."

The woman spotted Elaine.

"You."

"Good evening, Dahlia."

"He needs sleep. It's bad when he naps in a poetry seminar. That makes *all* of us look bad. You wouldn't understand that, Elaine."

"Honey, honey," Dr. Sohn said. "I'm fine. We're fine."

"And who is this?" Dahlia pointed to Jean. "Some homeless girl you brought into my house?"

"Maybe we should be going," Elaine said.

"I'd say look in *Sonic Review*, *Pulsatwaney*, and *Matterhorn Review*," Dr. Sohn said as Elaine and Jean made their way to the door. "I used to read those, but they aren't in the database."

With a few hours to kill before the library opened, Elaine and Jean drove to the Route 40 diner and had a big breakfast. Jean poured most of a bottle of syrup on her pancakes.

"Does it pay a lot?" she asked. "Being laureate?"

"No. No. Oh, no. God. No. Are you wondering how I can afford a feast like this?"

"You don't teach, right? How do you get by?"

"I'm sort of a detective."

"And people pay you? Because I can't."

"Sometimes people pay me. Usually they don't. I'm also pretty good at betting on college basketball."

Jean had nothing to say in response to that, so she ate everything on her plate and all of Elaine's bacon.

In the library, they found the old periodicals section and worked their way back through magazines that hid inside cheap leather. They started eight years ago then headed deeper into the past. To Jean the letters were like little bits of cereal on the page. She wasn't confident that she'd catch the phrase if she saw it, but Elaine worked efficiently and finally after two hours, she found it in a ten-year-old issue of *Sonic Review*.

"Hello, my friend."

It was there in a poem by a woman named Ruth O'Dowd who had attended Wesley College in Dover ten years earlier. She currently worked for a medical billing company in Chicago. They called to tell her how much they loved her poem.

"Sarah, sweet and stealthy," Elaine said. "That's a really interesting line. Do you remember where it came from?"

Ruth laughed. It sounded like she was walking on a crowded street, maybe on her way to work.

"Mark, the guy I was dating when I wrote that poem, he used to say it to me."

"Even though your name wasn't Sarah?"

"Yeah. He'd just learned the word *stealthy*, and he really wanted to use it. Like in a sentence."

"Was he a poet?"

"He seemed to think that anyone could just pick up a pen and call himself a poet."

"He was a good-looking guy, fit?"

"Oh, yes."

"You have any pictures of him?"

"Why are you so interested?" For the first time Ruth's guard went up. It was time to level with her.

"We think he stole something from my friend."

"Yeah," Ruth said. "He stole from me also. About fifty dollars and all my olive oil."

"Just ran off?"

"I met him in a bar one night, he basically moved in for a month. Then he took off."

"What was his last name?"

"Ulanger. He didn't tell me that, but I took his license out of his pants one time. This was maybe ten years ago. Such a funny time. I wore these sweaters, and I sat out on the steps and wrote poems in a little notebook. I was kind of a wreck, but also I looked down on everyone, everyone who wasn't me."

She sent them a picture of Mark. It was a bad, one blurry side shot, but you could see the kind of charm he put out there. This was their man.

"Maybe it was worth 50 dollars," Ruth said. "The sex was all right. I don't really use olive oil. I got one line of poetry out of it."

Mark Ulanger was as an assistant manager at a store in Indianapolis called Houseware Needz. It looked like he worked until closing on a Wednesday night.

"So he's gone straight?" Jean asked.

"It would appear," Elaine said. "If we leave right now, we should be able to make it."

The ride was nearly ten hours. Along the way Jean found a newspaper article from eight years earlier about a genuine Rheinspahn table abandoned in a courtyard outside a New Haven apartment building, warped and worthless.

She also found a website where Mark Ulanger posted an ever-expanding narrative poem about a young man riding across the country on a motorcycle, bedding women, cooking meat over an open fire out in the desert, teaching children how to whittle with a Bowie knife, playing dominoes with elderly men. He liked to describe sounds in detail. Like a campfire: *cruh-crack*. Or a horse trotting: *clip-a-clop*. Or sexual penetration: *squeesha-squeeesh*. Jean was able to follow most of it, but she didn't think that meant it was good.

Elaine had Jean check on basketball scores of the previous night. She'd gone six-and-five.

"That barely even covers the vig."

It made Jean angry that there were so many words she didn't understand. Even a tiny word like vig was completely foreign to her. She seemed to remember a time when she was much smarter, much more alert. There was also a time when she didn't need to wipe her dripping nose constantly, and all she had was a shredded tissue dug out from deep in a jacket pocket. When they stopped for gas, Elaine bought a new box of Kleenex.

"Sometimes I think I should be grateful to him," Jean said. "In a way he liberated me."

"How do you feel now?"

"I feel like he stole a table and ruined my life."

They made it to Houseware Needz about an hour before closing. It wasn't crowded, and they spotted Mark right away, standing in an apron, helping a woman find the right ceramic pear. There seemed to be more extra chit-chat between them than necessary: *we've also got some truly excellent salad bowls*. He mimed the shape of a truly excellent salad bowl, and the woman nodded enthusiastically. Finally she went to checkout, and Jean moved in on Mark while Elaine hung back two steps.

"Samson," Jean said.

"Sorry, my name isn't Samson," he said with a sunny smile.

"I just want to talk."

Quick vague recognition came into his eyes.

"Do you want me to stay?" Elaine asked.

"No. I can do this."

Jean spoke with real conviction, and Elaine went back to the car. Mark didn't admit to anything, but he gestured Jean to the cutlery section that same old, lazy forefinger.

"I don't really need an apology," she said.

"So why are you here?"

"Look at my hand."

She spread her left hand on a solid metal table.

"Okay. What am I looking at?"

"Now you. Put your hand out like this."

He paused a moment, but then complied. "Why not?" His hands were large and veiny. She remembered how strong they were. When she grabbed a cleaver from the display and brought it down on his forefinger, she was surprised how neatly it severed. She put it in her purse. She was out the door before the commotion began behind her. The car was parked around the corner.

"All right. I'm all done."

Elaine waited until they were back on the highway to speak.

"What did you do?"

"I cut off his finger."

"Is it in your purse?"

"Do you want to see it?"

"No, I don't."

"Do you think I did the right thing?"

"Well, it can't be changed now."

They drove another ten minutes.

"Where should I leave you?" Elaine asked.

"I don't see that it matters too much."

The Poet Laureate of Delaware left the girl in Cincinnati with 20 dollars, three Luna bars, and a purse that was beginning to drip. One drop just before she shut the car door: an image Elaine could use, that justified the whole night.

The *Houseware Needz Slashing* was well-covered in the Midwest. The prints off the knife were good, but they didn't match anyone in the system. There was no footage of the actual attack, only some blurry shots of the girl on her way in and then again on the way out. It was an eye-catching story for a few days, but it wasn't a murder or even an attempted murder. The investigation died out fairly soon. But exactly three months later, a nine-fingered man was appointed Poet Laureate of Indiana.

◇◇◇◇◇◇

With Hair Blacker Than Coal

Chris McGinley

◇◇◇◇◇◇

Sometime in the 1940s, a young mother in Burley County gave birth to a baby girl. The mother was only in her teens, just a girl herself, and the shame of it was too great to be borne, especially around the little hollers of eastern Kentucky, the way people gossip and judge there. On top of it, the no 'count father was long gone by the time the baby came. The girl felt she deserved *sympathy*, not condemnation.

And so she did the only thing she knew to do. She hiked up Red Thrush Mountain one day and left the child in the woods. That night, she claimed the baby had been stolen from her crib. The sympathy she wanted came in spades, but it only lasted a day or so. An old granny woman who had helped with the birth sensed the girl was telling a lie. She grabbed her by the hair and slapped the truth out of her. Soon a party of lawmen, the girl, and the granny woman were all headed up the hill to see if the baby was still alive.

There was a tiny feed sack dress on the ground where the baby had been left, covered in feline hair. But it hadn't been torn, and there was no evidence of blood anywhere, though bobcat prints were all over the place.

The baby had disappeared altogether.

Over the years the story became a part of the local folklore, the details changing according to circumstance. But the core of the tale remained the same. The baby had been raised by bobcats, people said. They talked of a wild girl who roamed high up in the woods on Red Thrush Mountain, making her lair in caves and rotted out logs. As time went on, the girl of the story became a woman, a feral animal, not to be approached under any conditions. Like all mountain stories, there were other ones that helped to prop it up. One time a team of geologists working for the mining company found a deer skin, stretched and tied with sinew to a stick frame. The site was miles away from any area trafficked by even the most adventuresome outdoorsmen. The group claimed to have seen bare footprints there, too, narrow ones. Another time a mountain spelunker swore he found evidence of someone living deep in a cave, though he could never again locate the entryway. And there were many supposed sightings by hunters. A filthy, naked girl running wild through the dense brush. A girl wearing skins and carrying a fire- hardened spear. A wild-looking girl who walked with bobcats, her hair a tangled nest grown to the waist, blacker than coal. Most of the stories were dismissed for what they were, fantastical accounts with little basis in fact. But others were more believable, according to the source, and the story persisted.

◇◇◇◇◇◇

To get to Indian Trace, Sheriff Curley Knott had to drive through the deep holler in Cyclops, a forlorn place that seemed never to end. He steered the cruiser around sharp twists and over rises, past run-down single wides that should have been abandoned, and between old coal company row houses about to fall over. Here and there someone sat on a rickety porch or leaned over the hood of a car. Mostly he got unwelcome stares.

At the back of the holler, a steep road with switchbacks that threaded through high limestone walls led the way to an old couple's homestead just below the Trace. The husband explained that he had heard a shotgun blast up on the rise behind the cabin a day earlier, and then another one seconds later. When he went to investigate he found two godless-looking men, harvesting a dead bear. "I told them boys there were two problems with what they was doing," he said. "First one is, it ain't bear season. Second one is, they was on my property without permission."

"What did they think of that?" the sheriff asked.

"The long haired one said I forgot about the third problem, that neither of them give a goddamn about number one nor number two. Said they was actually doing me a favor by leaving me the bear meat. But that if I didn't want it, they'd as like to kill me for being an ungrateful sonuvabitch. The other one pointed a gun at me and laughed. It was them Clatter brothers. I seen them up here before. They must've come across the bear just by luck. Bears are pretty rare around here. They mostly stay up above that notch. High up there. That's where them boys are headed, I think."

She had been quiet up until then, but now the old man's half-Shawnee wife chimed in. "That meat's befouled by them two. I wouldn't touch it. I said let the buzzards have it." She shook her head mournfully.

"Ok," the sheriff said, "let's go take a look."

The couple led the sheriff to the kill site, not too far from their little cabin. But about twenty yards from the animal, the old woman stopped short. "You all go ahead," she said. "I seen it once. And I wish

I hadn't." The men went on without her. As they neared the animal, Curley could see the red and black gore that clotted the high grass around the carcass. He had seen hundreds of dead animals in his time, had killed many himself, in fact. But there was something profane about the black bear that unsettled him. For one, the paws had been removed. The old man said he watched Cornelius Clatter take an axe to the animal. The hide, too, had been harvested, but the meat was left to rot on the bones. Flies swarmed around the carcass in a continually moving black cloud. Smeared with blood, the animal's sharp teeth sat open wide in an agonizing howl.

"By God this is strange," Curley said.

"It's unholy is what it is. It ain't natural," the old woman shouted from back on the path. Curley wondered how she had even heard him.

When they returned to the cabin, the man said that he didn't want the Clatter brothers arrested so much as he wanted them to stay off his land. He feared them, yes, but he feared more for the animals. In fact, the old man said, he'd not have made the report at all, but the woods high above Indian Trace were home to plenty of black bear nowadays, and he knew that the Clatters would likely come through his property again, killing and defiling.

"They're unclean," the old woman swore, pointing a crooked finger at Curley, who now noticed her high cheekbones and near black eyes. "They're a pox on these hills. I only hope they go too far. Beyond that notch up there is where they're headed. There's bear dens up there, and God knows what else. Don't follow them too far, sheriff. What's up there can't tell between good and not good. That's a dark wood up there, is what my grandfather called it. Anyone that hunts up there is just as like to be hunted. You be careful."

◇◇◇◇◇◇

After he radioed in, Curley outfitted himself with the hiking boots and light gear he kept in the cruiser. He was probably the best tracker in the county, but he didn't need to be. The Clatters took no pains to cover their tracks—cigarette butts, beer cans, shit and toilet paper. Not far from the bear kill, he came across a heavy canvas bag hung high in a tree. It dripped fluids and had already begun to stink. He figured it to be the hide and paws, and whatever else the Clatters had harvested from the animal they happened upon at Indian Trace. Curley wondered how the brothers ever got close to an animal, the way they hunted. But they were headed far up, beyond the notch. Surely they'd camp beforehand and start out early, using better cover, he thought. He hoped he would find them before then. Actually, part of him hoped he would never find them at all. He wasn't thrilled about going beyond that notch.

The fact was, the more he thought about it, and the further he hiked and the closer he got to the notch, the more he felt an impulse to turn around. He couldn't help but remember that time in the Mekong Delta. He wished he had turned around then, him and Brody. The two of them had to scout a remote area near a channel bank before a search and destroy mission. There hadn't been reports of any activity there, but they needed to be sure. According to Brody, it was supposed to be a half-hour in the woods, a "fuckin' nature hike," he said.

Problem was, the area didn't match up with the map. They followed a tributary upstream, through dense palm trees and mangrove roots, but it seemed never to end. At length, Curley began to feel it. Not the enemy. It was different than that feeling. It was something else, something of the jungle, something primal.

At one point, an animal moved in the trees up ahead of them, a large mammal, Curley figured. It let out a low, guttural moan. The sound was foreign to Curley, but he couldn't mistake the meaning. Brody readied to fire, but Curley shook his head. "There's no people out here," he whispered. "None thats alive, anyway." They backed out of there, turned around and headed for the rally point. But it wasn't long before they realized they were off the map again, on a different route from the one they took earlier.

"Fuck," Brody said. "We're lost." And Curley didn't counter him.

When they came upon it, they were already deep in the bush, wandering aimlessly. Against a felled durian tree lay a dead VC, his gun on the ground, the body shredded and disemboweled by something clawed, with deep incisors. And then they heard the rustling again, behind them now, and the low moan. When they stopped moving, the noises stopped, too. They were being followed, Curley realized. At times, they were afraid to move an inch. "There ain't but one way to do this," Curley finally said. "And you ain't gonna understand it, Brody. But you gotta trust me."

It was nightfall when they finally got back to the rally point. They had left their rifles on the banks and floated down the tributary for God knows how long, maybe a few miles, trying to stay close to the mangroves. Brody thought it was crazy to abandon the weapons, but Curley swore it was the only way.

Something was out there.

It was a long trek over rough terrain, a steep grade, and some muddy patches, but when the time came it wasn't hard to get the drop on Cornelius. Up high on the hillside, the sheriff could smell smoke from a little camp he figured to be about a mile away. When he finally got eyes on the situation, he circled back around and drew down on the older brother from behind. "Nothing sudden, ole boy," he said.

Cornelius sat on a fallen chestnut on the edge of a tiny clearing. He didn't move except to drag on a cigarette. "You here about that bear?" he asked. "'Cuz we got bigger problems, Law Man."

"Turn and face me."

"You said 'nothing sudden.' I'm just following orders."

"Turn around, Cornelius."

Cornelius forced a mirthless laugh and spun around on the tree trunk to face the sheriff. His stringy hair, matted with sweat across his forehead, fell almost to his shoulders. A lower tooth was missing. In one hand he held a cigarette and in the other a pint of Early Times. "I killed that bear on that old man's property," he said. "Poached it, I guess you call it. I don't mind to be arrested for it neither. But I got business up here first." He looked the sheriff up and down. "You're Curley Knott, right?"

The exchange wasn't what Curley had expected. "Where's that brother of yours?" he asked. Curley scanned the area around the camp, his gun still drawn. Cornelius took a deep breath, and Curley noticed the red in the man's eyes. Cornelius ground out the cigarette, pulled hard on the bottle and then replaced the cap. "Here," he said, tossing the bottle to Curley. "Take a snort. You'll need it for what I'm gonna show you." Curley thought it better to wait than to ask just yet.

Cornelius stared up into the tree canopy, but whether to ponder one of the big questions or to keep the tears from falling, Curley didn't know. One thing was for certain. Something was wrong with the man. A turkey vulture swooped down from an opening above and landed on a low branch across the tiny clearing. Cornelius tore a piece of decayed wood from the chestnut and threw it at the bird. "Get on out of here, goddamnit." Then he dropped his head into his hands and began to cry. Softly at first, and then with some real volume. In time he started to convulse, his shoulders shaking.

Curley had seen this before. Had been there himself, in fact, in the Delta. He needed details, but Cornelius had begun a mourning wail Curley knew better than to interrupt. He scanned the area again and took up a rifle that lay against the log. For a long while he waited, standing there, his eyes on Cornelius. At one point he actually thought to comfort the man, but he just couldn't. The act would have taken him back to the Delta, and that he couldn't do right now.

Finally he asked, "What happened, Cornelius?"

He had to wait a long while for a response, but eventually Cornelius rose from the fallen tree. "It's this way," was all he said. Curley followed at a distance, his gun still drawn, but it wasn't Cornelius he was worried about anymore. Something bad had happened. Curley could feel it, even more so the further they moved along. They crossed several fallen trees and wound their way up through a series of sandstone boulders. It was tough going. "We're headed toward the notch," Curley said at one point.

Cornelius kept moving, silently. They hiked for over an hour.

William's body lay at the base of a wide sycamore not too far from the edge of the notch. "He come out here to scout out a route," Cornelius said. "And because he liked to be alone in the woods, I guess. Anyway, he said he wanted to go alone. He was like that." Cornelius asked the sheriff if he could have the bottle again. Curley tossed it to him and moved to look over the body.

"Sweet Jesus," Curley said. The neck and torso had been raked deep by something with claws. And Curley saw some puncture wounds, too, from sharp canines. But nothing seemed to be ripped away. The flesh wasn't torn or shredded, though the ground was covered in blood, and flies buzzed everywhere. Curley looked for animal hair on the body, but he couldn't find any, and it vexed him. He felt the heat rise up inside of him, like that time in the Delta with Brody and the dead VC. He felt something else now, too, something feral in the air. Then, in the distance, he thought he heard a woman's cry, shrill long notes on the air.

"That's a bobcat," Cornelius said. "By God I will skewer that bitch."

"A bobcat didn't do this," Curley said. "This is something bigger. Maybe a mountain lion, or a bear. But not a bobcat."

The feminine cry sounded again, a long and desperate keening. Curley looked for prints in the area, moving carefully all around the body now, and out from it in a circle. He had to sit down when he finally saw it, on the other side of the tree. He would have fallen down otherwise. In the soft mud were narrow human footprints.

They led away from the body, toward the notch.

◇◇◇◇◇◇

Back at the camp the sheriff said, "It's just a goddamn myth, Cornelius. There's no wild woman on Red Thrush. The prints were made by something else. Have to be. They just look human. We'll get some people up here and remove his body tomorrow, or the day after. Right now, we gotta get moving. We gotta get down the mountain, all right?"

Cornelius had opened another pint of whiskey from a backpack and had been drinking from it since they had got back at the camp. Curley really didn't think he had cause to stop him.

"I'm too fucked up to hike back down there now," Cornelius said. "We'll go tomorrow morning, first thing."

It wasn't the way Curley wanted it, but what could he do? An injury on the descent could be dangerous. He could end up with *two* dead brothers. And he had to consider the reaction of the Clatter clan. No doubt, they would look to blame the sheriff's department if Cornelius got hurt. And God only knew what that would bring on. No, it was best to stay the night and move out early. Curley even took a few pulls off the pint. "You need to be ready to hike out right after sunrise," he told Cornelius.

Cornelius nodded and looked toward the path they had taken to get to the body. "You ever hear the story about that scientist who come up here to study on coal seams and excavation for one of the companies? Then he got separated from the rest of his crew somehow?"

Curley shook his head. "There are lots of stories. All just stories. People around here . . . you know, that's just part of mountain life. Tall tales."

Cornelius pulled on the bottle and passed it to Curley. "Yeah, but this guy. He never come back down. My cousin worked for the company back then. He said they sent guys up there looking, but they never found a trace of him. Creekside Mining Company. Long time ago."

Curley sipped on the bottle. "Lots of people gone missing in these hills over the years. Accidents happen. People get lost. That sort of stuff. Could be any number of things. What's a bunch of scientists know about mountaineering anyway? You send people like that up here, you're bound to have trouble."

"Hmm. Maybe so," Cornelius said. He got quiet all of a sudden and Curley hoped the matter had been dropped. A barred owl sung out from a tree some- where in the distance and something small rustled it the brush by the camp.

"Still, them footprints," Cornelius said.

Curley let out an exasperated breath. "Animal tracks, man. That's all."

"Maybe," Cornelius said. A light breeze shook the leaves in the canopy above and the owl sounded again. "You know, you and I could go investigate tomorrow. We got food. Hell, William's not gonna eat his share." He laughed at the realization, but Curley knew he didn't find it funny. "We could go across the notch and see what we find. I mean, we got a dead body up there. Ain't you supposed to look into that, sheriff?"

Curley said, "No. Your brother was not killed by a human being. He was mauled by some animal, or a pack of animals. That's not the business of the sher- iff's department."

Cornelius dragged on his cigarette. "Since when did that ever stop you? Most stuff gets investigated by the sheriff's department ain't the business of the sheriff's department, you ask me." He flicked the ash on the ground. "I think maybe you're scared of what's beyond that notch."

Curley took a last pull off the bottle and screwed the cap on. He passed it over to Cornelius. "Cornelius, some old people call that place a dark wood. They say that what's on the other side of that notch should be left alone. People oughtn't to venture out there, they say."

Cornelius took a drink. "Hell, you're scared, sheriff."

Curley pulled William's sleeping bag up high on his shoulders and settled in. "You're goddamn right I am."

Shafts of grey light had begun to poke through the trees and a wood pecker had started his work somewhere close by.

"Ain't no point in taking the tent and this other shit if we're just coming back up here to get William's body," Cornelius said. " Let's get going. Time ain't on our side, right?" He was already packed up and ready to move out. Curley was a little surprised. He took Cornelius for more of a slow-starter.

"Ok, give me five minutes," Curley said.

"Story of the po-lice. We'll be there when we get there."

Curley let it slide. He didn't need a conflict with Cornelius at this point, and as soon as he had his things together, the pair began to walk out, with Curley leading the way. He hadn't quite got up to pace yet and Cornelius let him know it.

"You're a little stiff there, sheriff. Come on, now. We gotta move, right?"

"I'm movin'. No sense in making a mistake way up here."

Cornelius laughed. "Hell, I thought you was supposed to be some kind of bad-ass mountaineer." Curley didn't like it, and he made a mental note to run Cornelius ragged when they got close to the bottom.

Less than a quarter mile from the camp there was a little drop through a sandstone crevice where the footing was tough. Cornelius passed in front and said, "You best let me lead here, sheriff. It's a little trickier than the training course down at the sheriff's academy." He laughed.

Forbearance wasn't always Curley's strong suit. He grabbed Cornelius' backpack and halted him in his tracks. "Watch how it's done, Jethro," he said. But as he was about to descend into the crevice, he heard Cornelius rustling around for something in his pack. He knew then he had made a mistake. Before he could turn around, he felt a sharp pain at the back of his head. He was only alert long enough to curse himself. And he only knew he had been kicked from behind when he awoke some time later, halfway down the crevice. His head and kidney throbbed, and blood covered his shoulder and back. His weapon was gone now, too, and Cornelius had taken the food and water. The only good thing was that the bleeding had stopped.

"Goddamn," Curley said. "Son of a goddamn bitch."

He knew he'd eventually arrest Cornelius and put him away, once he got down from the mountain, that is. And he could handle the small embarrassment of it, too. The smart thing to do, especially without food or water, was to hike down, call for backup, and wait out Cornelius at the base of the mountain.

But smart didn't always figure in.

Once he got his bearings, Curley started back up the mountain. His head and back ached, but as he began to move ahead, he felt a little energy slowly returning, helped along by his rising anger. At the camp, he collected the dew from the tent into a small pool and drank it down. William's Bowie knife was still there, in his bag, and he threaded the sheath onto his belt. It was early yet and he drizzled the dew from pawpaw leaves and other trees into his mouth as he moved. He figured Cornelius to be maybe an hour or so ahead. He also figured Cornelius had not intended to kill him, but just to abandon him so that he could hunt whatever it was that killed his brother, across the notch. Even so, would Cornelius take a shot in his direction, to ward him off? Maybe. He'd have to be careful.

When he got to a point just beyond William's body, Curley began to question the wisdom of his decision. The notch on Red Thrush was about eighty feet across and forty deep, with a steep drop. It required some technical footwork and some real strength. But by now he was thirsty again, and he hadn't eaten anything except some wood sorrel and Autumn olives. Again, he thought about turning around. But he saw where Cornelius had started across the notch. The track was right there in front of him.

He started down.

Just as he thought, the navigation was tricky but Curley came up on the other side in under an hour. He picked up Cornelius' trail on the other side and followed it through ever-thicker and thornier brush, navigating some rock formations and small crevices along the way. But after a few hours of circling back around and re-tracing his steps, finding and then losing the trail again, he realized that Cornelius was not to be found. Curley had lost the trail once and for all. He also realized that the longer he fumbled around up there, the more dangerous things would get. A brief rain allowed him to collect some more water, but he was in no great shape to keep on going.

It was then that he decided to cut his losses and head back. He had made several trail markers en route, but he couldn't find any of them now. It was as if they had been removed. Finally he decided to climb to the top of a limestone boulder to see if he could get a better vantage point. When he got to the top, all he saw was forest in every direction.

And then he sensed it. Just as soon as he got down from the boulder. A feral note on the air. He felt it in his mouth when he inhaled. There was a musky, animal smell to it, but something else was there, a scent he couldn't place, underneath the animal scent. He headed back in the direction he thought he had come, moving with more urgency now, the sound of cicadas making a loud din everywhere around him.

It startled him when he first saw it, though it shouldn't have, and he had to tell himself that a dead squirrel was not at all uncommon in a forest full of birds and larger mammals. It was recently mutilated, the meat torn from its small bones. Its guts lay there, covered in flies. Further along was a raccoon, and then a woodchuck. Next was a deer, a good sized buck whose neck had been thrashed and snapped. Bloody bobcat prints led away from the animal and the smell of feline urine was all over the air now.

Curley kept moving, he hoped in the direction of the notch, charging through the brush where it was thick instead of looking for a navigable path around. His hands and face soon became a mass of welts and cuts. He stopped short when he thought he heard something behind him, a rustling in the brush. But when he stopped, whatever it was stopped, too.

"Cornelius, is that you?"

Only the cicadas answered.

There was no getting around it now. Deep in the woods across the notch, he was hopelessly lost. Insects buzzed and leaves shook high up in the canopy. But Curley could feel no wind on the forest floor. Somewhere high above a red tail cawed, but when Curley looked up all he saw were turkey vultures. They circled and dipped, gliding above him easily and without concern, their wings barely moving. They had the advantage now.

Curley drew William's knife from its sheath, but to what end, he really didn't know.

◇◇◇◇◇◇

The details are hazy. At times Curley can recall large fragments of it, sometimes in dreams, or when he's out in the woods by himself. But he doesn't know whether or not he can trust them. His memory gets sharper the moment he emerged from the woods, dehydrated and famished, at the foot of the mountain near the old couples' cabin. The woman, the half-Shawnee wife, tended to him. He told the couple about how he confronted Cornelius at the camp, and about William's death at the hands of a bear, or maybe a mountain lion. Later he would lead a team up there to extract the body. But like the old woman when she saw the dead bear the Clatters had mutilated, he would hold back from the actual site itself.

◇◇◇◇◇◇

Curley told the old couple that he camped with Cornelius and planned to bring him back out the next day. But Cornelius had gone on before daybreak without telling him, no doubt intending to cross the notch and kill whatever animal took his brother's life. He must've gotten lost on the other side of the notch. Without food or water, Curley said, it would have been stupid to go after him. Instead he waited at the camp for hours. His own injury, he explained, was caused by a fall on the way down. The old man took him at his word, but the wife knew it was a lie. She knew Curley had gone across the notch, to the dark wood her grandfather had warned about. She knew something had happened there, too. She could still feel it on Curley's skin when she tended to him. But she also knew it was better not to ask. For both his sake and hers.

Nowadays, the story all changes around in his dreams. Sometimes the memory comes on the heels of a flashback, the details shifting and moving, even flowing back and forth between the Delta and Red Thrush.

But this much is true. Or at least Curley believes it to be.

When he first came upon Cornelius' body, the scene reminded him of some prehistoric cave paintings he had seen in a book once, as a little boy. The images had fascinated him then, a mixture of photographs and artist's renderings of the people who lived 50,000 years ago. He had turned the pages with both excitement and fear. There was something compelling about the way people had lived, Curley felt, close to the animals, close to danger. There was something primal about it, too, something irresistible, and he felt it then again as he looked at the mutilated body.

Cornelius lay near the low mouth of a cave surrounded by bloody paw prints on the rocks and in the dirt. The prints emanated out from his body, almost in concentric circles, but not so regular a pattern as that. It was a marker, Curley felt. Something claimed, something not to be disturbed. There was a set of what looked like human prints, too,

narrow ones, red at the balls and toes. And Curley could smell the strong feline urine again, along with that other scent he still couldn't place. Cornelius' mouth was locked in a silent scream, the missing lower tooth more pronounced now that his lips had been ripped off. Curley saw his own gun on the ground, but he knew better than to take it. Instead, he left William's knife there, placing it gently on the ground by the blade, the grip facing the cave door. He backed away from the opening, slowly, only turning to move ahead once he was well away. At one point on his way out he heard a noise, the feminine cry of the bobcat again. He turned to look back. In the dark mouth of the cave he saw the slow, feline movement of several animals at once. They swarmed over and under one another, in a serpentine dance of sorts. A buzzard landed near the body but quickly screeched and darted off, its wings working hard just to get airborne. Something else moved in the cave mouth then, but it disappeared just as quickly.

It looked like a long tress of black hair.

◇◇◇◇◇◇

She Goes First

Mary Thorson

◇◇◇◇◇◇

New York, 1928

Lula couldn't remember when Tom started discreetly coming to and leaving their bed, but there must have been a particular day when he decided to be quieter. It didn't matter, she was such a light sleeper that it wasn't the bird or the phone call that woke her, it was the absence of his weight. When she came into the kitchen, he was moving very fast, almost so her tired eyes couldn't keep up with him, and he blurred as he paced from one spot to another. Lula pulled her hair behind her ears and watched him. It had been a long time since she had seen him like this, and she was nervous.

"Who was on the phone?"

"Work, they want me for something big up in New York," he said over his shoulder.

"New York? Why?"

A few months ago, they had moved into their DC apartment from his studio in Chicago. Tom had said it was too cramped for him there, and there was an opening at the DC bureau of the Chicago Tribune. But Lula didn't think it was any bigger, now. Just emptier. The only furniture being the bed, a couch in the living room, and a kitchen table set that came cheap because it had been scratched in the store.

"You know that big case where the woman killed her husband? The dumbbell murder?"

Lula shook her head, she didn't pay attention to the news, which Tom had liked at the start. She knew it made him feel good to tell her about things.

"They're executing them next week and they want me to come in and take pictures."

"Pictures of what?"

"The execution," he said with a too big smile. "Just her, though. They're going to run it on the front page."

"You can't be serious," she said. "You mean, when she dies?"

"Mmhmm."

"Why would anyone want to see that?" Lula asked while letting her vision blur as she stared out the window. The snow was coming down in big heavy flakes as a few men in dark jackets started to make their trek to work.

"People can't not look," he said.

He would be working for the New York Daily News, he explained, because no photographers were being let into Ruth Snyder's execution, just reporters. The editors thought it would be clever to bring someone in that the guards had never seen before. They hired another man to make them a camera special for the job. The body of it would be strapped to Tom's ankle, the lens facing out and angled up, and the shutter release would be wired up through his pant leg to the arm of his jacket, so he could press it as if he were clicking a pen. It was single use.

She turned to look at Tom. His face was always astonishing. Hard set features, nothing soft there, not even his lips. A nose that had been broken more than once and eyes set deep. He cut into the space around him.

"That's sinful," she said.

If he could have left earlier, if the Daily News would have let him stay in one of their kept rooms at a hotel in the city, he would have been gone already, but they made him wait. Lula could sense him vibrating underneath his skin. He could see an exit.

"What about the bird?" Lula asked.

"What about him?"

"Do you expect me to take care of him?"

"Actually, yes. I do," Tom said. "It's not hard."

He walked over to the cage and let the bird out onto his finger. The bird twisted its head around to stare at her. Its neck bent unnaturally, and it made her put a hand up to her throat. Tom stroked it and whispered something that Lula couldn't hear.

The bird loved Tom. It was his bird. Well, not to start with. To start with it belonged to her. His wife's bird. During the divorce Lula and Tom had gone on an adventure; that's what he'd called it. They went to the house he had shared with her and broke in. He hadn't planned on it being dramatic as all that, but Margaret had changed the locks like she said she would. A rock the size of his fist got them in. One small broken window above the basement and it became something else.

Lula remembered the way Tom looked at her as if heat burned through his eyes. He helped her down and slid his hands over the length of her, touching every part. When her feet were flat on the ground, he held her there in front of him, against him. And when Lula turned, he had her there – it was the last time it went like that.

They walked right out the front door with the bird still in its cage and that black sheet over it. An African Grey. He had bought it for Margaret in place of an engagement ring. This bird looked as though all the color had been drained from him, everything but the tail which fanned out in a stark red cape. Lula liked the idea of getting Margaret's declaration of love as if it could be transferred over like money in a bank account.

Turned out Margaret couldn't stand the thing either, because she never came after it. Never said a word about it, and she always had a lot to say. This, Lula knew, had gotten under Tom's skin. He was excited the first few days, waiting to hear from Margaret once she came back to town. Said she would fight like a wet cat for that bird. Then the week rolled over to the next. He would ask if she called. Lula would ask why he cared, but she knew. Back in the beginning, when he and Lula had just started, he had told Margaret that the love bites on his neck were from the bird. But the bird never bit him.

◇◇◇◇◇◇

She read whatever she could find on Ruth and her lover. She hoped she could somehow learn more about them than Tom. Have an intimate insight into their lives that Tom wouldn't be able to capture and show. Ruth was 32. She was unemployed. She was a mother. Her daughter's name was Lorraine. Her husband's name was Albert. She and her lover, Judd, had killed him. Judd was a corset salesman and losing money. Ruth and Judd held chloroform soaked rags over Albert's mouth and nose. Judd tied a wire around Albert's neck. Judd convinced Ruth to do it so they could be together. Ruth convinced Judd to do it so they could be together. Ruth and Judd had been lovers for two years. Ruth and Judd turned on each other in two hours. All of it Lula memorized.

She wanted Tom to quiz her. She wanted him to bring something up, or get something wrong, and if he did, she would gently correct him. "No, that's not what happened; it went like this," she would say. And he would thank her. But Tom didn't talk about it. He just kept checking his backup camera and taking pictures of the bird.

◇◇◇◇◇◇

She had trouble sleeping when he was gone. Even though they had turned away from each other, his weight in the bed was enough. If not enough, something – a pull she could feel. A reminder in phys- ics. After Tom left, Lula ticked through those facts at night. When she did sleep, she dreamt of Ruth and Judd – but then it wasn't Judd, it was Tom. They stood in a room that had been torn apart, and he stood behind her, tying up her corset before he left. He kissed her in the space between her shoulder blades, grabbing her shoulder as if he wanted to take a part of her with him. Lula would wake up sweating. It reminded her of before. He would do this with Lula when her breathing got caught up and uneven. He would touch her with a kind of determined pressure. He had an agenda. He pawed at her while attempting to disguise it as comfort. He wanted.

But, over time, that pressure she needed had eased. He wouldn't touch her with any of his strength. She braced herself, ready to push back harder against him, but there was nothing. Quickly his hand would be gone altogether, leaving no imprint of where it had been. She used to be able to feel him the next day. Her hips would ache, and she'd stretch until she could feel the soreness. He bruised her neck with his mouth, and she'd open her collar up to the mirror as she examined the marks. Now he didn't leave anything behind.

◇◇◇◇◇◇

The day that Tom was due back, Lula woke up in the early afternoon, and the bird was squawking. She put the pillow over her head to try and block it out, but it didn't work. She threw the covers off of her and walked to the kitchen to make some coffee. She would not address the bird until she was ready. She would make it wait. When the coffee was ready, she poured it into a little white cup with delicate pink and blue roses on it and a gold painted trim around the rim. Lula had not bought this, it was not her style. She liked plain things—sturdy things. The bird squawked again. It was hungry. On her way out of the kitchen she tripped on the leg of the table, dropping her coffee cup on the ground. The thing seemed to shatter in slow motion, and she didn't move to stop it. The handle flew off like it had torn along a seam.

◇◇◇◇◇◇

"Shit," she whispered sharply.

"Shit! Shit!" came back at her from the living room.

The noise the cup made when it fell sounded like it came from inside her skull, and she put her hands over her ears. Lula stepped around the ceramic pieces and walked into the living room, balling up the folds of her robe in her fists. If she kept them free, she'd be liable to swing.

The bird heard her coming, and the cage started to shake. The black sheet with white embroidered vines covered it as it rocked back and forth. A heavy thing, made so the bird wouldn't be able to knock it off on its own.

"Please," Lula said, putting her mouth to the sheet. "Will you please, just, be quiet? I need you to do this for me. Can you? Please?" She breathed out, thinking maybe the hot air from her lungs would do something, like a car in a garage.

"Please! Please!" came from behind the sheet, like a ghost.

The bird's voice came out differently, this time. It sounded more like her, or how she thought she might sound to someone else. Desperate. Something was wrong with it. She wanted to be away from the bird, away from that voice, so she quietly walked to the front door hoping that it wouldn't hear her leave. When she stepped outside, the sun hit her as if interrogating her, and she sank down on the stairs. It was cold and she held her coat tightly to her chest. Her feet were bare but she was testing herself. It was a game; how long could she stand it. She would turn around to keep them moving, and was facing the navy blue door when she heard a car pull up in front of the house. She lifted her head and watched him. Tom paused for a moment, staring at her. He looked as if he'd gotten out at the wrong place. He kept his hand on top of the taxi, then he smiled and reached inside his coat. He pulled out a small bunch of crushed red roses and shook them her direction. He hit the roof and started towards her.

"What are you doing out here?" This was a thing he used to laugh at, but now it was a quick smile. She would have missed it if she had blinked. Thank God.

"I was hot, inside."

"You shouldn't be out here like this."

He opened the door and herded her through it. Inside, the bird started up again. Tom walked over, pulled off the sheet like a magic trick and leaned in.

"Hiya, buddy!" he yelled.

Lula put her hands up to her ears, fearing that her voice would come back out of its beak, but it was silent.

"There's a good man." Tom opened up the wire door and stuck his finger in. The bird marched onto it from its little swing. It flapped its wings and jumped onto Tom's shoulder, then stomped around a bit before settling down. Glad to be home.

"Seems a little stir crazy, must have gotten up early," Tom said, looking from the bird to Lula. His stare was accusatory.

"Excuse me," she said. "I need to wash up."

In the bathroom, she sat on the lid of the toilet with her hands between her knees. She leaned her head against the frosted window, and appreciated its coolness. Lula put her hand to her mouth and started to pick at the dry pieces of skin on her lips. Then she thought about lipstick – if she still had that color he used to like, or if he had ever mentioned liking one in particular.

Lula walked back to the kitchen and stopped in the doorway. She curled her toes to grip the floor. Tom had started another pot with the mess on the floor just inches away from his feet. He had the newspaper tucked into his waistband the way a cop carries a gun. She didn't want to ask about it, but had nothing else to say.

"How did it go, then?"

He turned and smiled at her, the kind of smile she hadn't seen in months. She almost returned it. He grabbed the newspaper and unrolled it. He held it up next to his face as if he were posing with some big game he had hunted.

"Take a look."

Lula couldn't understand at first. It wasn't something she could easily make out. She squinted her eyes causing the pain in her forehead to spread up underneath her hair and across to both temples. She became dizzy. In the picture, Ruth Snyder grabbed both arms of the chair with a grip that she never could have managed before that moment. Her ankles were straining against the leather strap, her feet kicked out to either side. She was wearing black loafers; Lula had a similar pair. Something black covered Ruth's face; it looked like a muzzle made for dogs. The photograph was blurry, and Lula couldn't tell if that was because she could actually see the electricity moving through Ruth's body or if it was the way the picture had been taken. Every sharp line in the photograph couldn't hold its content, the blacks and grays of her were bleeding out. At the bottom of the picture, there was something hard and shiny. A shoe. Tom's shoe. It looked so large and invasive. Right above the photo was a single big, bold word: DEAD!

"You ever seen anything like that?"

"Of course not." Lula rocked a little, placing one cold hand on the wall for balance. She felt as if she had been attacked.

"Here, take a look." Tom brought it close to her face, and she put her hands up.

"Look! Look!" the bird yelled out.

Lula sat down, and Tom grabbed the flowers he had set on the table.

"I'm sorry about these," he said. "They looked more alive when I got them." He started to poke through the petals, seemingly trying to find something in between them. Lula could feel the silk coming off on her fingertips.

"You shouldn't touch them," Lula said, louder than she had meant to.

A rigidness set in his shoulders at the sound of her voice, and she could see his jaw clench.

"What was it like?" she asked.

She saw him relax, and he turned back with a slight smile.

"Fast," he said. He pulled out a chair and sat down hard.

"The guard checked us." His hands were suddenly on her, moving up and down her sides. Lula took in a sharp breath. "Patted us down and let us in the room. I thought he would feel the wire, but you could tell they wanted to get that door closed. Press went to the back of the room, but I shoved up for a good spot where I could see her. Then they brought her in. You could tell she was scared; her lip quivered," he said as he moved his lip with his finger. "And her eyes were wide as planets, but she wasn't crying. They sat her down, strapped her in, then shaved the top of her head."

"Why?" Lula put her hand on top of her own. She imagined a draft.

"They put a wet sponge there." He tapped the top of her head, and she could almost feel her brain shake. "Makes the electrocution go faster, more humane."

"Did she say anything?" she whispered.

"'Forgive them father, for they know not what they do.' Then they flipped it. She grabbed hold of the chair with everything she had, then she went limp. I almost didn't get it in time, but everything lined up perfectly, thank God."

"Thank God." Lula repeated it back to him, slowly but reflexively. She couldn't help herself.

Lula stared at him as he looked over the picture—he couldn't stop smiling. He had caught something special, someone's soul on the outside of their body. He had caught it for himself, and it ignited him. There was nothing in the room now, not even him. He was still there, with Ruth.

"I felt bad for Judd Gray. When they brought him in you could still smell something, like metal. He was weeping and tripping over his feet when they sat him down. She went better than him; that's why they had her go first. They knew she would be better."

"I don't like it," Lula said.

Tom looked at her as if she had hit him.

"She wasn't a saint, you know." He crossed his arms over himself and hardness set back in.

Lula thought Ruth might have been, at the very least, some sort of martyr for herself. Everything had been taken from her and burned up.

"She only had dignity in dying, and that's what I got here."

It was quiet for a moment and then the bird squawked, making Lula's heart jump.

"Can you please get rid of that damn bird?" she said, putting her hands over her ears.

Tom stroked the bird's neck with his finger, then got up from his chair.

"I'm tired," he said with his eyes down. He didn't say anything else right away. The way he had said it sounded almost like a question that she should answer, the way it hung there between them. When he finally did look at her, she stopped breathing, wanting to be as quiet as possible.

"I like the bird," he said, before he turned and walked away.

TOUGH

Tom had left the bird on the table. Lula watched it and thought about how stuffy the room felt and how hot it had gotten with the sun coming in. She thought about opening a window while she scratched at her neck. The bird jumped down from the table to the ground so clumsily it surprised her. The bird couldn't fly – its wings were regularly clipped – but she didn't know if it even knew how. It walked over to the puddle of coffee on the linoleum and, with its beak to the floor, stuck its dry, gray tongue out, stabbing at the coffee in a way that made Lula feel sick again.

She had the newspaper in her hand. She didn't know how it got there, really; she must have grabbed it. The paper was thick – special issue heavy. She felt weak and swimmy, but she moved fast. Maybe faster than she had ever moved in her life. She got him on the first swing, and it made a terrible noise. A sort of scream that tried to be human but failed and cracked back into something else. It went on like that until it was over. She wished to God it couldn't talk, because even in the silence, with Tom looking at her in the doorway, wet and naked from the shower, she could still hear it ringing in her ears. Lula wondered if that's why they muzzled her.

◇◇◇◇◇◇

CPSIA information can be obtained
at www.ICGtesting.com
Printed in the USA
BVHW030230091220
595253BV00027B/245